SIMPLE FAITH

CHARLES R. SWINDOLL

Simple Faith

WORD PUBLISHING
DALLAS LONDON VANCOUVER MELBOURNE

WORD PUBLISHING 1996

Unless otherwise indicated, Scripture quotations used in
this book are from the New American Standard Bible (NASB)
© 1960, 1962, 1963, 1968, 1971, 1972, 1973, 1975, 1977
by The Lockman Foundation. Used by permission.

Other Scripture quotations are from the following
sources: The New English Bible (NEB), Copyright © the
Delegates of the Oxford University Press and the Syndics of the
Cambridge University Press, 1961, 1970. Reprinted by permission.
The New Testament in Modern English (PHILLIPS) by
J. B. Phillips, published by The Macmillan Company,
© 1958, 1960, 1972 by J. B. Phillips. The Revised Standard
Version of the Bible (RSV), copyrighted 1946, 1952, © 1971,
1973 by the Division of Christian Education of the National
Council of the Churches of Christ in the U.S.A., and are used by
permission. Scriptures identified as KJV are from the
King James Version of the Bible.

Book design by Mark McGarry
Set in ITC Bodoni

LIBRARY OF CONGRESS CATALOGING-IN-PUBLICATION DATA
Swindoll, Charles R.
Simple faith / Charles R. Swindoll.
p. cm.
ISBN 0-8499-3969-0
1. Christian life – Biblical teaching. 2. Faith – Biblical
teaching. 3. Sermon on the mount – Criticism,
interpretation, etc. I. Title.
BS2417.C5S85 1991
248.4–dc20 91-28519
CIP

Printed in the United States of America

6 7 8 9 0 9 OPM 6 5 4 3 2 1

Early in the spring of 1971,
a handful of men acted in simple faith.
The result of their decision was life-changing
for my family and me. They had been given the task of
finding a senior pastor to lead the congregation of
the First Evangelical Free Church of Fullerton, California.

Through a series of events
which called for much prayer and patience,
discernment and persistence, warm hospitality,
seasoned wisdom, and great grace,
they became the catalyst that God used
to pry me from a comfortable, familiar place
and call me to a stretching and challenging ministry
with potential beyond our fondest dreams.

As my wife and I sat with these men recently,
reflecting over the past twenty years,
we realized how much we owe each person.

Except for one—Walt Herbst, who passed into the Lord's
presence in 1988—all are still actively involved in
the church, and all are still within the circle of our
faithful friends, whom we love dearly.

Because they have modeled the message
of this book so consistently,
it is a privilege to dedicate it to them.

Irv Ahlquist	Emil Roberts
Bob Bobzien	Ray Smith
Walt Herbst	Phil Sutherland
Hamp Riley	John Watson

On the twentieth anniversary of our relationship,
I give God praise for their remarkable vision,
undiminished integrity, and simple faith.

Contents

Acknowledgments

NO BOOK I write is the product of one man's effort. While I may be the only one who researches all the material and puts the original words together, the process that precedes and follows those disciplines is a team effort, I can assure you.

I have my friends at Word Books to thank for their continued enthusiasm over my writing. People like Roland Lundy, Kip Jordon, and Ernie Owen have remained supportive and affirming in too many ways to mention. David Moberg has been especially helpful in designing the cover and arranging the layout of the book. Byron Williamson has, once again, proven the depth of his friendship by giving creative ideas and suggestions that motivated me when the task of doing another major volume seemed formidable. His tireless efforts and excitement over the project prodded me on during the long hours when I worked alone, surrounded by nothing but stacks of books and papers, half-finished cups of coffee, and silence. All of these friends, plus so many others in the Word family, deserve much of the credit that, unfortunately, will be given to me. To these people who have been the wind beneath my wings, I express my heartfelt gratitude.

I also wish to acknowledge the valuable assistance of Judith Markham, my editor on this volume. I am grateful for her attention to detail, her insightful observations and suggestions, and her enthusiastic commitment to this project. Amidst an already full schedule she agreed to work with me in getting the material book-ready before its deadline. Under her careful eye the manuscript was reshaped and crafted.

Those who know me best, however, realize that the most significant individual engaged in the process of any book I write is my long-term executive assistant, Helen Peters. Since I first put pen to paper, she has been there to bridge the gap between author and publisher. It would be impossible to describe all she does to turn my primitive-looking, handwritten tablet pages into a readable, pristine manuscript. Her patience in researching all the footnotes, her expertise in making the word processor hum, and her diligence in staying at the arduous and thankless task of presenting the final manuscript to my publisher ahead of schedule deserves an enormous round of applause. Thank you, yet again, Helen, for slugging it out night after night, page after page, with no loss of cheer or enthusiasm.

To my wife, Cynthia, I also express true gratitude,

especially for being so understanding of my intense love for writing. What began so many years ago almost as an afterthought has led to an addiction I cannot seem to break, nor do I try any longer. Instead of being jealous of it or selfish for my time, she is my most frequent source of encouragement. She listens as I read aloud one page after another. She interjects helpful hints when I cannot seem to get it said clearly. And she keeps on loving me and accepting my moods, even when my frustration mounts and I talk in my sleep . . . or jump out of bed at 2:30 in the morning when the ideas start flowing and my mind won't rest. Surely she must occasionally wonder if this isn't a bit more than she bargained for back in June of 1955 when we stood side by side and she said, "I do."

Finally, I am indebted to people like you, who pick up my book, thumb through its pages, and decide it is worth your effort to read it, and invest both your treasure and time to digest its content. Thank you sincerely. Just as music is meant to be played and sung, so a book is written to be read. Without your eyes and mind, my pen has little purpose, and apart from your trust, my writing is an exercise in futility. I suppose we could say that your decision to read this book is a matter of simple faith, for which I am grateful.

Introduction

WHEN I completed my previous volume, *The Grace Awakening*, I felt as if I had written the final words I wished to publish. In fact, I told several family members and friends that if I were suddenly taken ill and died, I would leave this earth a satisfied man—certainly a fulfilled author.

That volume was the culmination of decades of growth, thought, and struggle. It represented "my message" to the world—if a man can have one main message—especially to my immediate sphere of influence, the Christian community. For many years I had wished someone would write boldly and biblically about our freedom in Christ . . . about the stranglehold legalism has on many (most?) Christians . . . about the delights and discoveries to be enjoyed if folks would only get beyond the petty, man-made demands and restrictions of the grace killers and enter into a life that is free of guilt and shame, intimidation and manipulation. To my surprise, I wound up writing that book myself.

The response I received from readers has only reinforced my assumption: A multitude of people in religious bondage long to be free, and they have nothing but gratitude for anyone who will help them break the chains so they can run for daylight. I know; I have a file folder full of grateful letters. In all candor, I expected much more denunciation than appreciation. Instead, the opposite occurred. Much to my amazement, those who have been most grateful are pastors and other leaders in Christian ministries. The overwhelming majority who responded have communicated two specific things: (1) "Thank you for writing on grace. . . . I have determined to make a change in my life and/or my ministry," and (2) "Please write more. I need help in knowing how to put these desires into action." In other words, "Where do we go from here?"

This book, in many ways, is the result of such urging. (Since it obviously wasn't God's plan to take me home as soon as *The Grace Awakening* was published, I guess He wants me to keep writing.) While this is not, by any deliberate design on my part, a sequel to *The Grace Awakening*, it grows out of a similar passion within me: to help those who were once held captive know how to live the life Christ taught and modeled. The difference is that the people I have in mind for this book are those who have become victims of tyranny, not legalism. That tyranny is the pressure and frustration and disappointment brought on by the never-ending demands of organized religion. This kind of tyranny is intensifying because nothing in our world today is being simplified. In fact, everything in life has gotten complicated, including a life of faith. Instead of remaining a simple and meaningful relationship with God, the Christian life has evolved into a combination of big-time tingles, off-the-graph expectations, and borderline madness, which add up to voodoo religion.

Before you disagree, pause and ponder. Answer a few questions. Be painfully honest.

- Do you have a childlike trust in God?

- Are you comfortable with your prayer life?

- In a sentence or two, could you explain what it means to be a Christian?

- Does the word "satisfied" describe your feelings about your walk with Christ?

- Is "peace" the true condition of your inner being?

- Are you truly liberated from others' expectations?

- Have you been able to maintain a relaxed, contented, and joyful lifestyle in the midst of life's accelerated pace?

- If you were unable to attend your church for

several Sundays, would you feel comfortable, mildly uneasy, or guilt-ridden?

- Do you think the Bible can be understood by people who have not been to a Christian college or seminary?

- Can a person who is not a missionary be as spiritual as one who is?

- When you sin, do you know how to find forgiveness and continue on in your Christian life?

See what I mean? Somehow, the complications of life in general have bled into our walk with Christ . . . and messed everything up. Ask the average believer a simple question like, "What does it mean to be a mature Christian?" and if you are lucky, about fifteen minutes later you'll get the complete, complicated answer. The list of qualifications does not end.

"Maturity? Well, for starters you need to be in church as often as possible, witness regularly, teach a Sunday school class, pray fervently, make hospital visits, write uplifting notes to the discouraged, tithe, memorize Scripture, attend a Christian seminar or two each year, go to your church's summer family camp, support and attend the week-long evangelistic crusade, send your kids to a Christian school—or, preferably, home school them—participate on several boards or committees, serve in the (pick one) nursery, church kitchen, neighborhood visitation outreach program, choir, summer missions project, or right-to-life campaign. In addition, if you are a *really* mature Christian, there is no place in your life for discouragement, no room for doubt, and no time for just plain fun. Faith is serious stuff. It's intense.

Enter: complications. Exit: joy.

How far we have drifted from Christ's original teachings on the simplicity of faith. I'll go a step further: How grieved God must be at our frenzied pace! We have turned a walk with God into a ruthless obstacle course, an exhausting marathon. We have added enormously heavy weights to the runners, and, as a result, many are opting not to enter the race at all. Frankly, I don't blame them. Who needs extra baggage when life is already too heavy?

All this reminds me of a funny story I heard recently about a man at Los Angeles International Airport who was worried about missing his plane. He had no wrist watch and could not locate a clock, so he hurried up to a total stranger and said, " 'Scuse me . . . could you give me the time, please?"

The stranger smiled and said, "Sure." He set down the two large suitcases he was carrying and looked at the watch on his wrist. "It is exactly 5:09. The temperature outside is 73 degrees, and it is supposed to rain tonight. In London the sky is clear and the temperature is 38 degrees Celsius. The barometer reading there is 29.14 and falling. And, let's see, in Singapore the sun is shining brightly. Oh, by the way, the moon should be full tonight here in Los Angeles, and—"

"Your watch tells you all that?" the man interrupted.

"Oh, yes . . . and much more. You see, I invented this watch, and I can assure you there is no other timepiece like it in the world."

"I want to buy that watch! I'll pay you two thousand dollars for it right now."

"No, it's not for sale," said the stranger as he reached down to pick up his suitcases.

"Wait! Four thousand. I'll pay you *four* thousand dollars, cash," offered the man, reaching for his wallet.

"No, I can't sell it. You see, I plan to give it to my son for his twenty-first birthday. I invented it for him to enjoy."

"Okay, listen . . . I'll give you *ten* thousand dollars. I've got the money right here."

The stranger paused. "Ten thousand? Well, okay. It's yours for ten thousand even."

The man was absolutely elated. He paid the stranger, took the watch, snapped it on his wrist with glee, and said "Thanks" as he turned to leave.

"Wait," said the stranger. With a big smile he handed the two heavy suitcases to the man and added, "Don't forget the *batteries.*"

That's exactly what it is like when we tell folks about all the things Christ offers. We speak of one pleasure after another: this blessing and that benefit . . . sins forgiven . . . peace within, joy without . . . strength amidst trials, hope beyond the grave. I mean, who wouldn't want all that? But the killer is what we *don't* tell them. The package includes unexpected extra baggage, and it is only a matter of time before the added weight will turn a life of simple faith into a life oppressed by the tyranny of the urgent.

But what if being close to God were simple? What if this thing called faith isn't as complicated as it's cracked up to be? And while I'm asking the critical questions: What if you could be liberated—I mean really *set free*—from all those expectations that organized religion and even a few of your intense friends heap on you? What if I could show you how to get rid of all the excess baggage? What if you could return to a life that doesn't require running double-time or maintaining a superspiritual standard based on a hectic schedule?

I have the feeling you'd be interested. But you'd also be suspicious, right? You're sure that before I finished I would be handing you a couple of suitcases that are part of the deal, right? Wrong. The life of faith was never meant to be complicated . . . and that's what this book is about.

In a sentence: If Christ's life of *liberating grace* brings you hope beyond the bonds of legalism, you dare not miss Christ's words of *simple faith* to help you live beyond the harassment of expectations. As you will discover in the following pages, the Christian life is not based on high-level performance but on quiet faithfulness, not on impressive works but on deep relationships. God came to our rescue while we were trapped in a dark dungeon of despair. He gave us what we did not deserve and could not earn. He freed us. By breaking the iron bars of sin, He opened the gates of hope. Grace awakened us to a whole new world. But where do we go from there? Having been set free, how do we live? What's next?

To the surprise of many, the life Jesus lived and taught so clearly is neither demanding nor complicated. I like to think of it as a life beyond the dungeon. Charles Wesley's vivid description comes to mind:

> Long my imprisoned spirit lay
> Fast bound in sin and nature's night.
> Thine eye diffused a quick'ning ray:
> I woke, the dungeon flamed with light!
> My chains fell off, my heart was free,
> I rose, went forth, and followed Thee.[1]

Christ, who came to set captives free, still offers a life worth living to those who have been liberated. It is a life that may not always be easy or comfortable, but one thing is certain: It is not all that complicated. As we shall discover from Jesus' own words, spoken on a mountain in the first century, it is a life of *simple faith*. To make it more than that is heresy.

Charles R. Swindoll
Fullerton, California

*Just as you received Christ Jesus
the Lord, so go on living in
him—in simple faith.*

Colossians 2:6 PHILLIPS

CHAPTER ONE

Let's Keep It Simple

WHEN it came to clear communication, Jesus was a master. Children and adults alike had no difficulty understanding His words or following His reasoning. This is remarkable because while He was on earth He lived in a society that had become accustomed to cliché-ridden religious double-talk. The scribes, priests, and Pharisees who dominated the synagogue scene in Palestine saw to that. They unintentionally made Jesus' simple style and straightforward approach seem all the more refreshing. When He spoke, people listened. Unlike the pious professionals of His day, Jesus' words made sense.

This was never truer than when He sat down on a hillside with a group of His followers and talked about what really mattered. Thanks to tradition, this teaching session has come to be known as the Sermon on the Mount—in my opinion, an unfortunate title. His words were authoritative but not officious, insightful but not sermonic. His hillside chat was an informal,

reasonable, thoughtful, and unpretentious presentation. He distilled an enormous amount of truth in an
incredibly brief period of time, and those who had endured a lifetime of boring and irrelevant sermons sat
spellbound to the end.

> The result was that when Jesus had finished these
> words, the multitudes were amazed at His teaching; for
> He was teaching them as one having authority, and not as
> their scribes.   Matthew 7:28-29

If we fail to understand the background behind that
statement, we will not appreciate the depth of His listeners' gratitude. In short, they were fed up with the
manipulation, the pride, and especially the hypocrisy
of their religious leaders. Long years of legalism,
mixed with the pharisaic power plays designed to in-
timidate and control, held the general public in bondage. Man-made systems of complicated requirements
and backbreaking demands shut the people behind invisible bars, shackled in chains of guilt. They could not
measure up; they could not quite keep their heads
above water unless they dog-paddled like mad . . . and
many were losing heart. But who dared say so?

Out of the blue came Jesus with His message of liberating grace, encouragement to the weary, hope for
the sinful. Best of all, everything He said was based on
pristine truth—God's truth—instead of rigid religious
regulations. He talked of faith—simple faith—in terms

anyone could understand. His "yes face" invited them in as His teaching released them from guilt and shame, fear and confusion. The Nazarene's authenticity caught them off guard, disarmed their suspicions, and blew away the fog that had surrounded organized religion for decades. No wonder the people found Him amazing! No wonder the grace-killing scribes and Pharisees found Him unbearable! Hypocrisy despises authenticity. When truth unmasks wrong, those who are exposed get very nervous . . . like the two brothers in a story I heard recently.

These brothers were rich. They were also wicked. Both lived a wild, unprofitable existence, using their wealth to cover up the dark side of their lives. On the surface, however, few would have guessed it, for these consummate cover-up artists attended the same church almost every Sunday and contributed large sums to various church-related projects.

Then the church called a new pastor, a young man who preached the truth with zeal and courage. Before long, attendance had grown so much that the church needed a larger worship center. Being a man of keen insight and strong integrity, this young pastor had also seen through the hypocritical lifestyles of the two brothers.

Suddenly one of the brothers died, and the young pastor was asked to preach his funeral. The day before the funeral, the surviving brother pulled the minister aside and handed him an envelope. "There's a check in here that is large enough to pay the entire amount you need for the new sanctuary," he whispered. "All I ask is one favor: Tell the people at the funeral that *he was a saint.*" The minister gave the brother his word; he would do precisely what was asked. That afternoon he deposited the check into the church's account.

The next day the young pastor stood before the casket at the funeral service and said with firm conviction, "This man was an ungodly sinner, wicked to the core. He was unfaithful to his wife, hot-tempered with his children, ruthless in his business, and a hypocrite at church . . . but compared to his brother, *he was a saint.*"

The boldness of authenticity is beautiful to behold, unless, of course, you happen to be a hypocrite. That explains why Jesus' words, which brought such comfort to those who followed Him, enraged the Pharisees. Although He never called one of them by name during His hillside talk, He exposed their legalistic lifestyle as no one had ever done before. Count on it: *They* knew what He was saying.

On the surface, Jesus' words, recorded in Matthew 5, 6, and 7, may seem calm in tone and basic in their simplicity. We can read them in fifteen or twenty minutes, and at first glance they appear to be nothing more than a gentle tap on the shoulder. But to those who had twisted religion into a performance-oriented list of demands and expectations, they were nothing short of a bold exposé.

When Moses came down from Mount Sinai centuries earlier, he did not bring Ten Suggestions; likewise, when Jesus delivered His message from the mount, it was no humble homily. To legalists His words represented a howling reproach that continues into the modern age. Jesus' words may be simple, but they are definitely not insipid.

JESUS' WORDS: A PLEA FOR
TRUE RIGHTEOUSNESS

Behind Jesus' teaching on the Palestinian hillside was a deep concern for those who had surrendered their lives to the tyranny of pressure that was light-years away from simple faith. Of special concern to Him was the possibility that some had gotten sucked into the pharisaic model of substituting the artificial for the authentic, a danger that always lurks in the shadows of legalism.

That is what leads me to believe that the major message of Jesus' teaching in this setting could be encapsulated in these five words He spoke: "Do not be like them" (Matt. 6:8).

Our Lord wants His true followers to be distinct, unlike the majority who follow the herd. In solving conflicts, doing business, and responding to difficulties, Jesus' people are not to maintain the same attitudes or choose the priorities of the majority. And for sure, we are not to emulate pharisaism. When Jesus teaches,

"Do not be like them," He really means it. Hypocrisy, He hates . . . authenticity, He loves.

Hypocrisy permits us to travel both sides of the path—to look righteous but be unholy, to sound pious but be secretly profane. Invariably, those who get trapped in the hypocrisy syndrome find ways to mask their hollow core. The easiest approach is to add more activity, run faster, emphasize an intense, ever-enlarging agenda. The Pharisees were past masters at such things! Not content with the Mosaic Law that included the Ten Commandments, they tacked on 365 prohibitions, as well as 250 additional commandments. But did that make them righteous? Hardly.

> For I say to you, that unless your righteousness surpasses that of the scribes and Pharisees, you shall not enter the kingdom of heaven.   Matthew 5:20

No, you didn't misread it; He said *surpasses*. You see, a busier schedule mixed with a longer to-do list does not equal greater righteousness any more than driving faster leads to a calmer spirit. On the contrary, when we attempt to become more spiritual by doing more things, we do nothing but complicate the Christian life. Can you imagine the shock on the faces of the Pharisees when they heard that Jesus was telling His followers that their righteousness must *exceed* that of the Pharisees?

In fact, if we do a quick overview of Jesus' magnificent message, we find Him simplifying the walk of faith with four basic teachings, all of which were diametrically opposed to the pharisaic lifestyle. First of all, He says:

Out with Hypocrisy!

Even a casual reading through the forty-eight verses in the fifth chapter of Matthew leads me to believe Jesus is answering three questions:

1. What does it mean to have character? (vv. 3-12)
2. What does it mean to make a difference? (vv. 13-16)
3. What does it mean to be godly? (vv. 17-48)

Interestingly, in that third section, verses 17-48, He repeats the same statement no fewer than six times:

"You have heard . . . but I say to you. . . ." (vv. 21-22)
"You have heard . . . but I say to you. . . ." (vv. 27-28)
"It was said . . . but I say to you. . . ." (vv. 31-32)
"You have heard . . . but I say to you. . . ." (vv. 33-34)
"You have heard . . . but I say to you. . . ." (vv. 38-39)
"You have heard . . . but I say to you. . . ." (vv. 43-44)

Why? What is Jesus getting at?
He is reminding the people of what they have heard

for years, taught (and certainly embellished!) by their religious leaders; then He readdresses those same matters with an authentic life in view. And what kind of life is that? A life free of hypocrisy. Jesus' desire is that His followers be people of simple faith, modeled in grace, based on truth. Nothing more. Nothing less. Nothing else.

How easy it is to fake Christianity . . . to polish a superpious image that looks godly but is phony. Through the years I have come across Christians who are breaking their necks to be Mother Teresa Number Two or, if you please, Brother Teresa! Or Saint Francis of Houston or Minneapolis or Seattle . . . or wherever. Far too many Christians are simply trying too hard. They are busy, to be sure. But righteous? I mean, genuinely Christlike?

Sincere? Many of them. Intense? Most. Busy? Yes...but far from spiritual.

Several years ago I came across one of the simplest and best pieces of advice I have ever heard: "Be who you is, because if you is who you ain't, you ain't who you is."[1] Wise words, easily forgotten in the squirrel cage of religious hyperactivity.

Down with Performance!

If the early part of Jesus' teaching is saying, "Out with hypocrisy," this next section, recorded in Matthew 6, is saying, "Down with performance!" Quit placing so much attention on looking good. Quit trying to make others think you are pious, especially if beneath the veneer there are hidden wickedness, impure motives, and shameful deeds. In other words, don't wear a smiling mask to disguise sadness and depravity, heartache and brokenness. In the area where I live, we would say, "Leave Showtime to the Los Angeles Lakers."

Jesus puts it straight: "Beware of practicing your righteousness before men to be noticed by them" (Matt. 6:1). In other words, "Stop acting one way before others, knowing you are really not that way at all." Then He offers three practical examples:

1. *Giving*

> When therefore you give alms [when you are in church and you give your money], do not sound a trumpet before you, as the hypocrites do in the synagogues and in the streets.   Matthew 6:2

Today, we don't blow trumpets—not literally. But many who give sizable contributions like to see their names cast in bronze. They like it to be known by the public and remembered forever that they were the ones who built the gym. They are the ones who paid for the new organ. They are the heavy givers . . . the high donors: "A little extra fanfare, please." In contrast, when it came to giving, Jesus emphasized anonymity. No more hype, He said. When we live by simple faith, big-time performances that bring us the glory are out of place.

What a wonderful and welcome reminder—unless, of course, you are a religious glory hog. When we choose a life of simple faith, we keep our giving habits quiet.

2. *Praying*

> And when you pray, you are not to be as the hypocrites; for they love to stand and pray in the synagogues and on the street corners, in order to be seen by men. Truly I say to you, they have their reward in full. But you, when you pray, go into your inner room, and when you have shut your door, pray to your Father who is in secret, and your Father who sees in secret will repay you. And when you are praying, do not use meaningless repetition, as the Gentiles do, for they suppose that they will be heard for their many words.   Matthew 6:5-7

Many words, even eloquent words, never caused anyone to be heard in prayer. My fellow preachers and I who are often called upon to pray in public would do well to remember that.

Dr. Lewis Sperry Chafer told a story on this subject.

> It seems that a certain minister was in the habit of profound prayers, oftentimes resorting to words beyond the ken of his simple flock. This went on week after week, to the dismay and frustration of the congregation. At last, a wee Scottish woman in the choir ventured to take the

matter in hand. On a given Sunday, as the minister was waxing his most eloquently verbose, the little woman reached across the curtain separating the choir from the pulpit. Taking a firm grasp on the frock tail of the minister, she gave it a yank, and was heard to whisper, "Jes' call Him Fether, and ask 'im for somethin."[2]

Whatever happened to simplicity in prayer? And uncluttered honesty? Like the prayer of a child. Or the prayer of a humble farmer needing rain. Or of a homeless mother with two hungry kids. Down with performance-oriented praying! God honors simple-hearted petitions and humble-minded confession.

3. *Fasting*

And whenever you fast, do not put on a gloomy face as the hypocrites do, for they neglect their appearance in order to be seen fasting by men. Truly I say to you, they have their reward in full. But you, when you fast, anoint your head, and wash your face so that you may not be seen fasting by men, but by your Father who is in secret; and your Father who sees in secret will repay you.   Matthew 6:16–18

This is a great place to stop and say a further word to fellow preachers. When it comes to piety performance, we can be the worst offenders! All preachers know there's a way to look and sound like The Reverend Supersanctified Saint of Ultrapious Cathedral or Dr.

Dull Dryasdust with stooped shoulders, long face, and dark suit (an out-of-date tie also helps) . . . struggling to keep the tonnage of his world in orbit and its inhabitants in line. There's a great Greek word for that kind of nonsense: *Hogwash!* Jesus shot holes in that look-at-me-because-I'm-so-spiritual showmanship. If we choose to fast, fine. In fact, it's commendable. But if we fast (or counsel or study or pray) to be seen, forget it! These disciplines were never meant to be displays of the flesh. We are not in them for the grade others give us or the superficial impression we can make. Leave the acting to those who compete for the Emmys and the Oscars. As suggested earlier, "Be who you is. . . ." Let's keep it simple. Out with hypocrisy! Down with performance! And:

Up with Tolerance!

I believe that is what Jesus is saying in the first five verses of Matthew 7. What searching, convicting words these are!

Do not judge lest you be judged. For in the way you judge, you will be judged; and by your standard of measure, it will be measured to you. And why do you look at the speck that is in your brother's eye, but do not notice the log that is in your own eye? Or how can you say to your brother, "Let me take the speck out of your eye," and behold, the log is in your own eye? You hypocrite, first take the log out of your own eye, and then you will see clearly to take the speck out of your brother's eye.

He is continuing His passionate, howling reproach against hypocrisy, isn't He? But have we taken Him seriously? Not nearly enough.

Christians are fast becoming "speck specialists." We look for specks and detect specks and criticize specks, all the while deliberately ignoring the much larger and uglier and more offensive logs in our own lives that need immediate attention and major surgery—in some cases, *radical* surgery.

May I get specific? Be tolerant of those who live different lifestyles. Be tolerant of those who don't look like you, who don't dress like you, who don't care about the things you care about, who don't relax like you, who don't vote like you. As my teenage kids used to ask each other, "Who died and put you in charge?" You're not their judge.

Let me go even further. Be tolerant of those whose fine points of theology differ from yours. Be tolerant of those whose worship style is different. Be tolerant even of those who have been turned off by Bible-thumping evangelicals—folks who are up to here with the pettiness and small-mindedness in many churches. Be tolerant of the young if you are older . . . and be tolerant of the aging if you are young. For those who are theologically astute (especially you who are gifted and trained linguistically), be tolerant of those who don't know Hebrew or

Greek. There is certainly nothing wrong with knowing those languages, you understand. They can be extremely helpful. But they can also be misused and abused. People who don't know the original languages of Scripture can be taken advantage of by those who do.

My close friend and pastoral associate, Paul Sailhamer, tells a humorous story that perfectly illustrates what I am getting at. Though apocryphal, it is appropriate.

Jorge Rodriquez was the meanest, orneriest bandit on the Texas-Mexico border. The guy would often slip across the line, raid the banks of South Texas, and steal 'em blind. Before they could catch him, he would race back into Mexico and hide out. No matter how hard the law tried, they could never catch him.

Finally the Texans got fed up with this nonsense and decided to put the toughest Texas Ranger they had on the case. Sure enough, that got the job done. After only a few days of searching, the Ranger found the bandit in a dingy, dusty saloon south of the border. He bolted into the bar, pulled both guns, and yelled, "Okay, stick 'em up, Jorge; you're under arrest! I know you've got the money."

Suddenly a little guy over in the corner butted in. "Wait, wait . . . just a minute, señor," he said. "Jorge does not speak English. He's my amigo, so I'll translate for you."

The Ranger explained, "Look, we know he's the

bandit we've been looking for. We know he's taken thousands and thousands of dollars—about a million bucks, actually. We want it back *now*. Either he pays up or I'll fill him full of holes. You tell him that!"

"Okay, okay! I'll tell him . . . I'll tell him." So the little fellow turned to Jorge and repeated in Spanish everything the Ranger had said. The Texas Ranger, not knowing a word of the language, waited for the bandit's reply.

Jorge listened, frowned, then responded in Spanish, "Okay, they got me. Tell him to go down to the well just south of town, count four stones down from the top of the well, then pull out the one loose stone. All the money I have stolen I've hidden behind the stone."

Then the clever little translator turned to the Texas Ranger and translated with a shrug, "Jorge says, 'Go ahead, you big mouth; go ahead and shoot 'cause I'm not telling you where the money is.'"

On with Commitment!

Jesus' words penetrate, don't they? When our faith is a genuine faith—a simple expression of our walk with God—tolerance comes more easily. But does this negate commitment? Does everything about faith become passive and mildly indifferent? Not at all. Take a look at the rest of Jesus' talk recorded in Matthew 7. Pay close attention to the commands. Here are a few of them:

Do not give what is holy to dogs, and do not throw your pearls before swine, lest they trample them under their feet, and turn and tear you to pieces.

Ask, and it shall be given to you; seek, and you shall find; knock, and it shall be opened to you. . . .

Enter by the narrow gate; for the gate is wide, and the way is broad that leads to destruction, and many are those who enter by it. . . .

Beware of the false prophets, who come to you in sheep's clothing, but inwardly are ravenous wolves.

Matthew 7:6–7, 13, 15

Now that's commitment! We will examine these exhortations and others much more carefully later in the book; but for now, don't kid yourself that living a life of simple faith means a yawn in the sunshine of convenience and casual commitment.

As our Lord brings His teaching to a close, He tells the story of two houses, one built on rock and another built on sand. And with this He wraps up His words with one major statement: *People of simple faith mean what they say and do what they hear.* That, in essence, is the practical outworking of Christianity. That is simple faith in a nutshell.

Unfortunately, we neither mean what we say nor do what we hear. We substitute words for action and pious discussion for personal involvement. As one writer put it:

> I was hungry
> and you formed a humanities club
> and you discussed my hunger.
> Thank you.
>
> I was imprisoned
> and you crept off quietly
> to your chapel in the cellar
> and prayed for my release.
>
> I was naked
> and in your mind
> you debated the morality of my
> appearance.
>
> I was sick
> and you knelt and thanked God
> for your health.
>
> I was homeless
> and you preached to me
> of the spiritual shelter of the
> love of God.
>
> I was lonely
> and you left me alone
> to pray for me.
>
> You seem so holy;
> so close to God.
> But I'm still very hungry and lonely
> and cold.

> So where have your prayers gone?
> What have they done?
>
> What does it profit a man to page through his
> book of prayers when the rest of the world is
> crying for help?[3]

Jesus' words that day on the hillside were even more powerful. When He finished speaking, nobody moved. Small wonder. Those words were like spikes, nailing them to their seats.

As A. T. Robertson writes:

> They [the people] had heard many sermons before from the regular rabbis in the synagogues. We have specimens of these discourses preserved in the Mishna and Gemara, the Jewish Talmud when both were completed, the driest, dullest collection of disjointed comments upon every conceivable problem in the history of mankind. . . .
>
> Jesus spoke with the authority of truth, the reality and freshness of the morning light, and the power of God's Spirit. This sermon which made such a profound impression ended with the tragedy of the fall of the house on the sand like the crash of a giant oak in the forest. There was no smoothing over the outcome.[4]

SIMPLY PUT: MY RESPONSE

We're only one chapter deep, but already I feel the need to make four statements of honest confession lest we "smooth over the outcome." If these represent *your* life, too, join me in admitting the truth. I believe it will stop us in our tracks and help us then take the first steps to a life of simple faith.

First: *I admit I am not completely free of hypocrisy.* I confess it, Lord, and I know I'm not alone.

> I am like James and John.
> Lord, I size up other people
> in terms of what they can do for me;
> how they can further my program,
> feed my ego,
> satisfy my needs,
> give me strategic advantage.
> I exploit people,
> ostensibly for your sake,
> but really for my own sake.
> Lord, I turn to you
> to get the inside track
> and obtain special favors,
> your direction for my schemes,
> your power for my projects,
> your sanction for my ambitions,
> your blank check for whatever I want.
> I am like James and John.
>
> Change me, Lord.
> Make me a man who asks of you and of others,
> what can I do for you?[5]

If you find yourself in those words, as I do, then you must admit there are often hidden agendas within you.

Second: *I admit I do not always search my motives.* I openly confess that I do not always ask myself *why.* Jesus' words never fail to force me to examine my motives. Do you find that true as well? As we get under way in this book, my hope is that God will search you and reveal to you whatever is impure yet remains hidden.

Third: *I admit I still occasionally judge others.* My intolerance is at times blistering; my pride, at times, rotten and putrid. My patience, so short. My acceptance, so limited. Is yours? Don't be afraid to say so. It is the truth that will set you free.

Fourth: *I dare not continue as I am.* That's a statement I need to make. Do you? We need help to change—to sift truth from error, essentials from incidentals.

Some years ago I was given a book of Puritan prayers called *The Valley of Vision.* I have worn out one copy and had to purchase another. Late this afternoon as I was putting the final touches on this chapter, which has become so convicting, I happened upon a page from the Puritan's pen. Because it says so well what I'm trying to say, I close with his words, not mine. Read them slowly, preferably aloud.

O LORD,
I am a shell full of dust,
but animated with an invisible rational soul
and made anew by an unseen power of grace;

Yet I am no rare object of valuable price,
but one that has nothing and is nothing,
although chosen of thee from eternity,
 given to Christ, and born again;
I am deeply convinced of the evil and misery of a
    sinful state, of the vanity of creatures,
but also of the sufficiency of Christ.
When thou wouldst guide me I control myself,
When thou wouldst be sovereign I rule myself.
When thou wouldst take care of me I suffice myself.
When I should depend on thy providings I supply
    myself,
When I should submit to thy providence I follow my
    will,
When I should study, love, honour, trust thee, I serve
    myself;
I fault and correct thy laws to suit myself,
Instead of thee I look to man's approbation,
and am by nature an idolater.
Lord, it is my chief design to bring my heart back to
    thee.
Convince me that I cannot be my own god, or make
    myself happy,
nor my own Christ to restore my joy,
nor my own Spirit to teach, guide, and rule me.
Help me to see that grace does this by providential
    affliction,
for when my credit is god thou dost cast me lower,
when riches are my idol thou dost wing them away,
when pleasure is my all thou dost turn it into bitter-
    ness.

Take away my roving eye, curious ear, greedy appetite,
  lustful heart;
  Show me that none of these things
  can heal a wounded conscience,
  or support a tottering frame,
  or uphold a departing spirit. Then take me to the
  cross and leave me there.[6]

CHAPTER TWO

The Qualities of
Simple Faith

GOOD SERMONS are rare; great ones, almost unheard of these days. Of the hundreds—perhaps thousands—some of us have heard in our lifetimes, precious few fit the category of "great." Chances are good that those were preached by humble servants of God. Great sermons and godly servants usually go together.

Reminds me of the young, gifted minister whose preaching was a cut above the ordinary. As the ranks of his congregation began to swell, his head followed suit. After he had delivered his latest barnburner one morning, one of his loyal parishioners earnestly shook his hand and said, "You're becoming one of the greatest expositors of this generation, pastor."

As he squeezed his head into the car and slid behind the steering wheel, his weary wife alongside him and all the kids stuffed into the back seat, he could not resist sharing the story.

"Mrs. Franklin told me she thought I was one of the greatest expositors of this generation," he said proudly, caught up in the heady swirl of the woman's exaggerated compliment.

No response.

Fishing for affirmation, he glanced at his silent wife with a weak smile and prodded, "I wonder just how many 'great expositors' there are in this generation?"

Unable to resist the opportunity to set the record straight, she said quietly, "One less than you think, my dear."

No greater message was ever delivered than the one Jesus spoke from the Galilean mountainside. No more humble messenger ever communicated the life of simple faith than that thirtysomething carpenter-turned-teacher from Nazareth. Twenty centuries have not come near exhausting its depths. With precision and courage He delivered one surgical strike after another, exposing the hypocrisy and legalism of first-century religion. As listeners followed His logic with mouths open in awe, they realized they were not sitting at the feet of another arrogant scribe but rather before the God-man, the Messiah Himself. Can you imagine the thrill of being there? To this day, His words strip away all the excess baggage many have added to the life of faith. It is a masterpiece of simplicity.

THE QUALITIES OF JESUS' DELIVERY

Having just read Matthew 5, 6, and 7 again, four general observations come to mind, each quite a striking contrast to the standard sermon preached today.

First: *He spoke these words outside rather than inside.* That means they were probably delivered extemporaneously and, for sure, without the aid of voice amplification. Perhaps that explains why He chose a hillside rather than a section of flat terrain in Palestine.

Second: *He was sitting down among His listeners rather than standing up before them.* His presence, while powerful, was not overpowering. By sitting with them, He remained approachable, touchable, believable.

Third: *He taught rather than preached.* His message had substance that called for action. Rather than relying on a series of emotional exhortations, He delivered teaching that was systematically and logically arranged. But make no mistake, His presentation was neither laid-back nor lacking in force. He taught them "as one having authority" (Matt. 7:29).

Fourth: *He blessed and encouraged rather than rebuked.* Most sermons are more negative than positive, more like scathing rebukes than affirmation. Not this one. With beautiful simplicity, using terms any age could understand, Jesus brought blessing rather than condemnation.

No fewer than nine times, back-to-back, He used the same phrase: "Blessed are those . . . ," "Blessed are you . . . ," "Blessed are these. . . ." Having endured a lifetime of verbal assaults by the scribes and Pharisees, the multitude on the mount must have thought they had died and gone to heaven. A pinch of positive blessing does more for our souls than a pound of negative bruising. When will we preachers ever learn?

THE QUALITIES OF THE BLESSED LIFE

As we dig deeper into these opening words from our Lord's message, we encounter one "blessed" comment after another. Here they are, exactly as Jesus delivered them. Though familiar, read them as if for the first time. Study His words with care. Notice the refreshing absence of clichés.

> Blessed are the poor in spirit, for theirs is the kingdom of heaven.
>
> Blessed are those who mourn, for they shall be comforted.
>
> Blessed are the gentle, for they shall inherit the earth.
>
> Blessed are those who hunger and thirst for righteousness, for they shall be satisfied.
>
> Blessed are the merciful, for they shall receive mercy.
>
> Blessed are the pure in heart, for they shall see God.
>
> Blessed are the peacemakers, for they shall be called sons of God.
>
> Blessed are those who have been persecuted for the

sake of righteousness, for theirs is the kingdom of heaven. Blessed are you when men cast insults at you, and persecute you, and say all kinds of evil against you falsely, on account of Me. Rejoice, and be glad, for your reward in heaven is great, for so they persecuted the prophets who were before you.   Matthew 5:3-12

What is meant by *blessed?* Some say it is little more than a synonym for "happy," but it is much deeper than that. In extra-biblical literature, the Greek term that is translated *blessed* was used to describe two different conditions. First, it was used to describe the social stratum of the wealthy who, by virtue of their riches, lived above the normal cares and worries of lesser folk. Second, the term was also used to describe the condition of the Greek gods who, because they had whatever they desired, existed in an unbelievable state of well-being, satisfaction, and contentment.

To be sure, Jesus was speaking neither to the wealthy nor to the gods of the ancient world. But by repeating the same word to His band of simple-hearted, loyal followers, He reassured them that enviable qualities such as delight, contentment, fulfillment, and deeply entrenched joy were theirs to claim. In other words, He promised that by tossing aside all the extra baggage that accompanies religious hypocrisy and a performance-oriented lifestyle, we will travel the road that leads to inner peace. In doing so, we become "blessed."

But let's not think of these beatitudes as a collection of insipid, trite remarks or mild, sentimental platitudes designed to make everyone smile. Jesus didn't offer feel-good theology. A close examination reveals that His opening words pose a frontal challenge to virtually everything we assume about the way things are in our world. Or, as G. K. Chesterton remarked, "Most critics who are offended at the things Jesus says are offended precisely because Jesus does not utter safe platitudes."[1]

Though simple sounding and easy to read, each beatitude offers a radical rearrangement of our ordinary value system, daring us to be different. What we find here, in short, are guidelines for true Christian character. In a day like ours where acting has replaced authenticity and pretense gets the nod over inward reality, I know of no greater need than this dose of truth.

"Blessed are the poor in spirit." Not poor in substance, but spirit. This first beatitude has nothing to do with being materially destitute or financially bankrupt. Jesus is placing value on a humble spirit, on those who acknowledge a spiritual bankruptcy in and of themselves. Where there is an absence of well-polished pride and personal conceit, there is a wholesome dependence on the living God. Instead of, "No problem, I can handle it. After all, look at the things I've accomplished already," there is quick confession, acknowledging one's own inadequacies.

Do you recall a contrasting scene Jesus created in

one of His parables? Luke 18:9-14 records the account of two men, one a proud Pharisee, nauseatingly impressed with himself, and the other an unworthy, tax-gathering sinner, too aware of his transgressions to speak above a whisper. The Pharisee stood praying to himself, his words dripping with arrogance,

> . . . God, I thank Thee that I am not like other people: swindlers, unjust, adulterers, or even like this tax-gatherer. I fast twice a week; I pay tithes of all that I get.   Luke 18:11b-2

Such pharisaic arrogance can be found in slick, proud-spirited, corporate-minded congregations . . . like the one in lukewarm Laodicea, a church in existence toward the end of the first century, mentioned in Revelation 3:14-18. Our Lord reproved the people of that church because they said, "I am rich, and have become wealthy, and have need of nothing" (v. 17a). But they did not realize that, spiritually speaking, they were "wretched and miserable and poor and blind and naked" (v. 17b).

In bold contrast to that whitewashed tombstone, the tax-gatherer described in Luke 18:13, painfully cognizant of his own lack of righteousness, was unwilling even to lift up his eyes to heaven. Instead, he pounded his chest as he muttered his simple, honest admission of need, "God, be merciful to me, the sinner!" The difference? The tax-gatherer was "poor in spirit."

Augustus Toplady captured the essence of this

poor-in-spirit quality in several lines of his great hymn "Rock of Ages":

> Nothing in my hand I bring,
> Simply to Thy cross I cling;
> Naked, come to Thee for dress,
> Helpless, look to Thee for grace;
> Foul, I to the fountain fly,
> Wash me, Saviour, or I die![2]

And the promised blessing for such a humble, dependent, poor-in-spirit attitude? "Theirs is the kingdom of heaven," Jesus said. By living lives of such simple faith beneath our Father's sovereign, gracious care, we truly enter into what kingdom living is all about.

"Blessed are those who mourn." This word translated "mourn" is the strongest Greek term the writer could have used to convey the idea of a passionate lament—the utter sorrow of a broken heart, a desperate ache of the soul. One who mourns enters into deep and intense anguish, whether mourning over something that is wrong and/or out of control in one's own life or in the world in general . . . mourning over some personal loss of possession . . . mourning over someone's death. In light of the context, it most likely refers to a passionate lament of the heart, something we might call a spirit of contrition. This is vividly portrayed by Paul in his statement of unguarded vulnerability at the conclusion of his description of his own spiritual turmoil:

"Wretched man that I am! Who will set me free from the body of this death?" (Rom. 7:24).

In a time of extremes like ours, when the glorious grace of our God is taken advantage of and misapplied to mean "live as you please," it is easy to make too little of our sin. How seldom do we find a contrite heart, or, as Jesus put it, how rare are "those who mourn" over their own wretchedness. Rather than mourning, many are "moaning" over the fact that other Christians don't look the other way and shrug off their sinful behavior.

To "mourn" is to acknowledge the overwhelming sinfulness of one's own sin, feeling indescribable sadness and brokenness over the wrong that has transpired. Like Peter, who, after denying his Lord on three separate occasions, felt the sudden weight, the enormity, of his transgression. His reaction? Scripture tells us, "And he went out and wept bitterly" (Luke 22:62). A similar scene occurs in Psalm 32 when David's sins associated with his Bathsheba affair led to "groaning all day long," which, in turn, caused his "vitality" to drain away (vv. 3-4). David mourned. Any attempt to rationalize or ignore wrongdoing only complicates matters. Simple faith calls for swift and complete confession. Those who mourn, Jesus promises, are blessed.

Sometimes our mourning is prompted by another's wrong. Recently my wife and I watched a segment of the popular television program "60 Minutes." It featured several men and women—mourners all—who are close relatives of some of Adolf Hitler's highest-ranking henchmen. The relatives' grief-stricken faces, their anguished tears, and their halting words told their own tragic story. Humiliated, embarrassed, ashamed, and heartbroken over their heritage, each expressed feelings of deepest lament. My heart went out to those tormented men and women, several near my own age, whose lives have been marked and marred by another's sin.

And what is it Jesus promises those who mourn, who refuse to ignore their sin? "They shall be comforted," He says. Wonderful reassurance! Elsewhere in Scripture the Lord promises to bind up the brokenhearted, to give relief and full deliverance to those whose spirits have been weighed down by the realization of their failure and wrong. Read the following promise, then rejoice:

> For Thou dost not delight in sacrifice,
> otherwise I would give it:
> Thou art not pleased with burnt offering.
> The sacrifices of God are a broken spirit;
> A broken and a contrite heart, O God,
> Thou wilt not despise.   Psalm 51:16-17

God does not expect or require months of misery-evoking penance or daily sacrifices to appease His anger. Christ's death on our behalf provided the once-for-all payment for sin. Nevertheless, a contrite heart that expresses itself in mourning over wrongdoing results in divine comfort. Count on it.

"Blessed are the gentle, for they shall inherit the earth." Read that again, only this time think of that statement being made by some sales manager today. Or try to imagine the words coming from a competitive boss: "Just be gentle with your customer, okay?" You're probably smiling. In our high-pressured world of aggressive techniques, gentleness suggests becoming someone's doormat . . . sort of a cross between a wimp and a wallflower. What an unfortunate distortion of what Jesus taught.

Gentleness, in its genuine and original meaning, was used in various ways, all of them admirable:

- A wild stallion that had been ridden, broken, and brought under control was said to be "gentle."

- Words that calmed strong emotions were "gentle" words.

- Ointment that drew fever and pain out of a wound was a "gentle" medication.

- In one of Plato's works, a child asked a physician to be *tender* with him. He used the same Greek word translated "gentle."

- Those who were polite, treating others with dignity, courtesy, and tact, were called "gentle."

Even Jesus, when disclosing His personality, spoke of Himself as being "gentle and humble in heart"

(Matt. 11:29). Obviously the word was used differently then than it is today. Rather than today's meaning of insecure, unsure, weak, or effeminate, back then it was a term denoting true inner strength under control. D. Martyn Lloyd-Jones adds this clarifying statement: "The man who is truly *meek* [gentle] is the one who is amazed that God and man can think of him as well as they do and treat him as well as they do" (emphasis mine).[3]

And what blessing did Jesus promise the gentle? "They shall inherit the earth," He said. That is not a reference to conquering and controlling the world. What it means is that, spiritually speaking, our needs will be met. As we trust the Lord to provide, we gain the "inheritance" He makes possible as He fights the battles and wins the territory. We don't have to roll up our sleeves and fight to the finish; He fights for us. We don't have to be preoccupied with protecting our rights or grappling for control; the Lord enables us to inherit whatever "land" we need. The greedy grab and lose, while the gentle inherit and gain.

What strange information in this era of demand for personal rights! Recently I saw a cartoon depicting a tiny baby only seconds after birth. The physician had the baby by the feet, holding him upside down and slapping him on the fanny. Instead of crying, the kid was screaming angrily, "I want a lawyer!" And so do most folks these days. The attitude is, "Who wants to wait for God to provide if I can sue someone's pants off and get what I want *now?*"

Are you serious about simplifying your walk of faith? Try gentleness. Allow your Lord room to be just that—the sovereign Lord in full control, capable of fighting for you and conquering whatever territory you need to inherit.

"Blessed are those who hunger and thirst for righteousness." This beatitude reflects true spiritual passion, an insatiable hunger to know God intimately, to model His ways personally. Don't misread this. Jesus is not talking about merely increasing one's knowledge of biblical or doctrinal facts, though there is certainly nothing wrong with that. Instead, He's talking about aligning oneself with God's character: holiness, truth, goodness, and righteousness. Included in this "hunger and thirst" would certainly be the cultivation of the discipline of prayer and waiting on God, the submission of the will, and the desire to weave all that into everyday living. This is not to be pushed to unreasonable extremes that require a man to become a monk. Nor is Jesus interested in turning a mother into some sort of dreamy-eyed seraph who quotes Scripture instead of fixing meals. "Hungering and thirsting" means taking God seriously and finding how perfectly His truth fits into real-world existence. Best of all, as with both physical hunger and thirst, this spiritual appetite is an ongoing desire, needing to be frequently replenished on a daily basis.

And what will happen to those whose longing for

God is so intense? Jesus promises, "they shall be satisfied." Wonderful thought! Rather than being perpetual victims of spiritual starvation, never getting sufficient nourishment to grow strong, "they shall be satisfied." One New Testament scholar suggests that the word "satisfied" was commonly used in reference to feeding and fattening cattle, since the root Greek term is the word for fodder or grass.[4] We have this hope: We will become so spiritually satisfied that we will be like hefty, well-fed livestock–strong, stable, able to handle harsh conditions and endure uncomfortable circumstances. Now that's a needed promise! God's pantry never runs low. His wells never run dry.

Interestingly, while the first four beatitudes focus attention on our relationship with the Lord–that vital vertical dimension of simple faith–the final four seem to emphasize the horizontal dimension, our *people-with-people relationships.*

"Blessed are the merciful, for they shall receive mercy." Mercy is a concern for people in need. It has to do with assisting those less fortunate than ourselves, including those who suffer the consequences of disappointment, disease, and distress. One of my mentors used to say, "Mercy is God's ministry to the miserable." And it does not stop with compassion or sadness over someone in dire straits; it means identifying with those who are hurting and imagining the pain they are having to endure, then doing something about it.

When I think of mercy, I usually think of the Good Samaritan, the traveler who stopped to help a man who had been mugged, robbed, and abandoned by the road. Several religious leaders had already walked by the injured man. Perhaps they were preoccupied with practicing their sermons, repeating their memory verses, or going over their impressive "to-do" lists for the day. At any rate, not one of them gave the battered man the time of day. Then along came the Samaritan. He stopped and put himself in the broken man's place. He took time. He cleansed the man's wounds. He even loaded the man on his donkey and carried him to an inn for the night. And he said to the innkeeper, "Put it on my tab."

That's mercy at its best. It's not simply some feeling of sympathy or sadness over somebody in trouble, but really getting inside the other persons' skin, feeling what *they* feel, understanding *their* misery, and then helping them through it.

And whenever I think of the Good Samaritan, I also remember a couple of other Samaritan-like passages:

> If a brother or sister is without clothing and in need of daily food, and one of you says to them, "Go in peace, be warmed and be filled," and yet you do not give them what is necessary for their body, what use is that? Even so faith, if it has no works, is dead, being by itself.   James 2:15–17

> But whoever has the world's goods, and beholds his brother in need and closes his heart against him, how does the love of God abide in him?   1 John 3:17

These verses pose some searching, probing questions: What good is unshared wealth? and, How does the love of God abide in such a person?

Shakespeare, in *The Merchant of Venice*, used these lines to describe mercy:

> The quality of mercy is not strained,
> It droppeth as the gentle rain from heaven.

Mercy is not reluctant. Force is not required to move it into action. No one has to hammerlock you and say, "Show mercy! Show mercy!" Mercy is voluntary. It flows like the gentle, falling rain.

What can we expect if we show mercy? Our Lord assures us in this beatitude that the merciful will, in turn, receive mercy. Those who live by mercy will die in mercy. You give to others in their misery, and they will give to you in your misery. God will see to it that your merciful investments today reap wonderful benefits tomorrow.

I know of no better setting in which to demonstrate mercy than in a marriage. Several months ago I sat behind a couple of newlyweds on a flight back to Los Angeles. How do I know they were newlyweds? Well, they were all over each other! He kissed her and she kissed him. She had left her purse in the overhead compartment, so she kissed him and asked if he would get it for her. He kissed her back as he stood up to get it. When he brought the purse down, it didn't look like it was worth all those kisses to me. But she kissed him again, and he kissed her back. I mean, they were so attentive to each other it was almost sickening! When the flight attendants served the meals, the bride kissed him before the meal . . . and he kissed her before, during, and after the meal. I had the same meal; it wasn't worth kissing over, I can assure you. It was just the usual "toy food" you get on an airplane—just another toy biscuit, toy meat, toy salad, and toy cake, plus a toy cup of coffee. Really, that stuff wasn't worth a kiss. As we arrived at the Los Angeles airport and everybody got up to leave, she reminded him with a kiss to pick up the things that were underneath the seat. After he pulled them out, he gave her a hug and another kiss! Soon they were walking out arm in arm. I confess, I was tempted to say in a booming voice, "I want to see you two in five years!"

It's not that you stop kissing; it's just that as life begins to unfold, things happen that require more than a quick kiss. You need to keep the fires of affection and tenderness stoked with something stronger. Heartaches happen, and that calls for mutual mercy. You are there for each other through the night. Both of you hang in there through the long haul. That's the kind of reciprocal give-and-take in the marriage commitment that calls for mercy. As one mate demonstrates it, God leads the other to reciprocate. As Jesus promised, the merciful will receive mercy.

"Blessed are the pure in heart." Simplicity and purity fit together beautifully. A life of simple faith is linked to a pure heart. Perhaps the words "blessed are the utterly sincere" would be an appropriate paraphrase. If a film were made about someone who lived this kind of completely sincere life in both private and public, there would be no need to edit. You could videotape that person at church or at home, at work or at play, and you would catch no contradictions. The pure in heart live transparently . . . no guile, no hidden motives. How seldom we encounter anyone who lives anywhere near that standard!

What we all too often observe is what John R. W. Stott portrays in these tragic words: "Some people weave round themselves such a tissue of lies that they can no longer tell which part of them is real and which is make-believe."[5]

Rare though the "pure in heart" may be, this beatitude implies that life *can* be lived without masks. "Blessed are the pure in heart, for they shall see God." Meaning? They will see God work. They will see Him in their lives. They will feel His presence. There will be no waking up in fear that someone is going to find out the real truth. There is nothing to hide. There is just the living of a life before the all-seeing presence of God. That is the way our Lord lived, and He happily offers it to us.

"Blessed are the peacemakers." Peacemakers release

tension, they don't intensify it. Peacemakers seek solutions and find no delight in arguments. Peacemakers calm the waters, they don't trouble them. Peacemakers work hard to keep an offense from occurring. And if it has occurred, they strive for resolution. Peacemakers lower their voices rather than raise them. Peacemakers generate more light than heat. Blessed are such greathearted souls! We need more of them in the ranks of faith. We have more than enough fighters, more than enough who are ready to pounce.

Make no mistake, however; *peacemaker* is not a synonym for *appeaser.* This is not peace at any price. There are limits. Just as Dietrich Bonhoeffer introduced the presence of "cheap grace,"[6] our Lord introduces the possibility of "cheap peace."

Cheap peace occurs when my brother (or sister) brings reproach to the name of Christ yet does not repent. For me to go right on as though everything is fine and dandy and, even worse, assure him he is forgiven and "all is well" cheapens peace. We are warned against that. Luke 17:3 says, "If he [your brother] repents, forgive him." It cheapens peace to ignore the gross offense, treat it lightly, and release him from accountability and responsibility if he doesn't have a contrite heart of repentance.

Churches are told to dwell together in unity, but not at the expense of sound doctrine. If a group is embracing heresy, you do not enhance the gospel by smiling and agreeing, all in the name of peace. Smiling at wrongdoing or erroneous teaching doesn't simplify life; it complicates it.

When Christ blessed the peacemakers, He was extolling the value of doing all we can to maintain harmony and support unity. His interest was in making peace where peace is an appropriate objective.

And what can peacemakers count on? "They will be called the sons of God," said Jesus. Was not Christ Himself called that by His followers? By our pursuing peace as He did, we shall be Christlike, sons and daughters of the living God, people with the Father's nature. So it is for those who choose to live in simple faith.

"Blessed are those who have been persecuted for the sake of righteousness, for theirs is the kingdom of heaven. Blessed are you when men cast insults at you, and persecute you, and say all kinds of evil against you falsely, on account of Me." Now let's be careful with this one. Note again the *reason* these folks are being persecuted: "for the sake of righteousness." There is a kind of persecution we bring upon ourselves because we have been discourteous or needlessly offensive. There are certain reactions we can arouse simply because we adhere to some fanatical extreme that is based on personal taste or private opinion. But that is not what Jesus has in mind here. True persecution occurs when two irreconcilable value systems collide.

When that occurs and you choose to stand on the principles of truth, you can count on it, *you will be persecuted.*

How will it happen? They will "cast insults at you," and "persecute you." The word translated *persecute* means "to pursue to the end." They will hunt you down. They will tell all kinds of evil lies about you. They will assassinate your character . . . and on certain extreme occasions, they may even attempt to take your life on account of Him. That has happened before, and it will happen again.

And how should you respond? "Rejoice, and be glad." Why? For two reasons. First, because "your reward in heaven is great." And second, because "so they persecuted the prophets who were before you." You are not alone. You are, in fact, in a long succession of very noble company. What a compliment!

When I go through this list of beatitudes, I am reminded all over again that God's ways are topsy-turvy to the world's ways. A few examples: God exalts the humble, but the world exalts the proud. God ascribes greatness, not to masters, but to servants. God is impressed, not with noise or size or wealth, but with quiet things . . . things done in secret—the inner motives, the true heart condition. God sends away the arrogant and the rich empty-handed, but He gathers to Himself the lowly, the broken, the prisoner, the prostitute, the repentant. The world honors the handsome and the gifted and the brilliant. God smiles on the crippled, the ones who can't keep up. All this makes the world nervous.

As Bonhoeffer once wrote: "And so the disciples are strangers in the world, unwelcome guests, disturbers of the peace. No wonder the world rejects them!"[7]

SIMPLY PUT: APPLYING JESUS' WORDS

How does all of this make sense for our daily lives? How do we develop this list of character traits with a view toward simple faith? In keeping with our theme, let's keep it simple. Here are two ideas.

Try this: Apply one beatitude a day. On Monday work on *dependence*, consciously focusing on being "poor in spirit." On Tuesday, apply *repentance*. On Wednesday, try *gentleness* as an attitude for the day. On Thursday, go after *righteousness*. Friday, let's make it a full day of *mercy*. Saturday, think on *integrity*. Sunday, deliberately be a *peacemaker*. And the next Monday? Cultivate *joy*. That will get you out of a repetitious cycle. Because there are eight beatitudes but only seven days in the week, you will have a new day with a new project on a regular basis. I challenge you: In place of a lifestyle that you have learned from the world's system, put these qualities into practice. Before you know it, your faith will begin to be simple again.

Here is another idea. Start listening for contrasts between the world's message and Christ's philosophy. You'll be amazed.

For example, instead of being a couch potato, start really "watching" television. Listen to what is being said. Better yet, notice what is *not* being said. Quit being gullible. How did the rich and famous get those lifestyles? Did they manipulate their way to the top? What about all those "honest," self-aware talk shows? Are they leading you to feed the flesh and encouraging you to fight selfishly for your own way? Think about the unending parade of award shows with their pride on display. Start paying close attention to what you are seeing and hearing. Keep in mind the Beatitudes and you'll witness many contrary messages emerging in seminars you attend and in magazines you read, as well as in the daily newspaper. But unless you're alert to these things, you'll be squeezed into the world's mold.

Ask the Lord to give you a redirection in life—to bring you back to simple faith.

I have often been grateful for the writings of J. B. Phillips, both his paraphrase of the New Testament and the volumes he authored. He has a way of capturing the essence of meaning in memorable words. He cleverly paraphrased the Beatitudes as the non-Christian world would prefer them. See if you don't agree that this version would fit rather well in today's media handbook:

> Happy are the "pushers": for they get on in the world.
> Happy are the hard-boiled: for they never let life hurt them.

Happy are they who complain: for they get their own
  way in the end.
Happy are the blasé: for they never worry over
  their sins.
Happy are the slave-drivers: for they get results.
Happy are the knowledgeable men of the world:
  for they know their way around.
Happy are the trouble-makers: for they make people
  take notice of them.[8]

The Teacher from Nazareth offers a better way:

How happy are the humble-minded, for the Kingdom of
  Heaven is theirs!
How happy are those who know what sorrow means, for
  they will be given courage and comfort!
Happy are those who claim nothing, for the whole earth
  will belong to them!
Happy are those who are hungry and thirsty for good-
  ness, for they will be fully satisfied!
Happy are the merciful, for they will have mercy shown
  to them!
Happy are the utterly sincere, for they will see God!
Happy are those who make peace, for they will be
  known as sons of God![9] Matthew 5:3–10

These qualities of simple faith, when put into action, result in a life worth living. I dare you to try it.

CHAPTER THREE

A Simple Counterstrategy:
Shake and Shine

ALMOST 275 years ago Isaac Watts asked three questions that need to be answered today. They appear in the lines of a hymn he wrote back in 1724, a hymn still sung in English-speaking churches around the world. Even its title is a question: "Am I a Soldier of the Cross?" But the questions I'm speaking of appear in the third stanza of that old hymn:

- Are there no foes for me to face?
- Must I not stem the flood?
- Is this vile world a friend to grace, to help me on to God?

Think about each of these, especially that last one; it's the clincher. Remove your rose-colored glasses. Toss aside your albums of dreamy love songs. Forget the motivational seminars and all those shoot-for-the-stars, positive-thinking, self-help paperbacks. Now then, looking at "this vile world" in raw reality, answer the question: *Is it a friend to grace?* Will this world help you to know God? Love Him? Serve Him? As you sit at the feet of its professors, as you listen to its music and watch its films . . . as you take your cues from its philosophy and model its media, will the road narrow to the path that leads to God? No one in his or her right mind could ever answer yes.

Ours is a hell-bound, degenerate world and you know it. Isaac Watts's word is timelessly true: *vile.* Political corruption abounds. Academic pursuits, though temporarily stimulating, leave graduates empty and on futile searches that never satisfy. International peace, a splendid ideal, continues to blow up in our faces as war recurs with painful regularity. The crime rate escalates as domestic violence and gang wars and drug traffic and overcrowded jails continue to plague society. Pending legal cases choke the courts of our land with an endless litany of litigation. And even when cases are finally brought to trial, no courtroom or prison cell can remove madness from minds or hatred from hearts.

THE PLAIN TRUTH ABOUT THE REAL WORLD

The world is a war zone full of foes that must be faced. If it were not for the reliable promises God has given in the pages of His Book, a spirit of fatalism would reign supreme. The battle would already be lost.

Too bleak? An exaggeration? You decide after reading these words from the pen of the Apostle John: "We know that we are of God, and the whole world lies in *the power of* the evil one" (1 John 5:19). Three words—"the power of"—appear in italics in the text. The editors of the New American Standard Bible have added these words to make the passage clearer. Let me suggest a further variation: "The whole world lies in *the lap of* the wicked one" (italics mine).

Satan, our relentless enemy, has a game plan, and it's on the board. Knowing that his days are numbered, knowing that he has an appointed amount of time before the scoreboard counts him out, he holds the world in his lap and gives it directions, implementing his strategy day after day. On the surface, his plays are impressive and appealing and even very satisfying . . . for a while. So long as the adversary can keep earth's inhabitants believing his lies and blinded to his schemes, he will continue his subtle strategy. But the truth is, his ploys work against everything that is holy and just and good. I repeat Isaac Watts's question: "Is this vile world a friend to grace, to help us on to God?" Indeed, it is not.

To affirm the truth of that simple answer, read John's earlier words from the same letter:

> Do not love the world, nor the things in the world. If anyone loves the world, the love of the Father is not in him. For all that is in the world, the lust of the flesh and the lust

of the eyes and the boastful pride of life, is not from the Father, but is from the world. And the world is passing away, and also its lusts; but the one who does the will of God abides forever.   1 John 2:15-17

Then who or what are we to love? Jesus' words come to mind: "This I command you, that you love one another. If the world hates you, you know that it has hated Me before it hated you" (John 15:17-18).

This raises another question: What can we expect from the world? We can expect *hatred* because the world hated the Lord Jesus Christ. And if we are in league with Him, it is going to hate us, as well.

Since this is true, what else can we expect from the world? *Persecution.* Jesus also warned of that during His earthly pilgrimage. "These things I have spoken to you, that in Me you may have peace. In the world you have tribulation. . . ." (John 16:33a).

What can we expect from the world? Hatred, persecution, tribulation. Those three reactions should never surprise us. They are not pleasant, for sure, but we have no reason to be caught off guard . . . or, for that matter, to feel abandoned or overwhelmed. Jesus went on to say, ". . . but take courage; I have overcome the world" (John 16:33b).

Why will the world treat us with hatred and persecution and tribulation? Two reasons: *generally* because the world lies in the lap of the wicked one, and *specifically* because we belong to Christ. It hated Him, so it will hate us. But therein lies the genius of our counterstrategy: By our being different, many in the world will realize what they are missing and will be drawn to Christ . . . a classic example of the old saying "opposites attract."

D. Martyn Lloyd-Jones is exactly right when he writes:

> The glory of the gospel is that when the Church is absolutely different from the world, she invariably attracts it. It is then that the world is made to listen to her message, though it may hate it at first.[1]

If our message is a mirror image of the message of the world, the world yawns and goes on its way, saying, "What else is new? I've heard all that since I was born." But if the Christian lifestyle and motivation and answers are different, the world cannot help but sit up and take notice, thinking:

- How come they live in the same place I live, but they are able to live a different kind of life?

- How is it that I cannot conquer this habit but he has?

- Why is their love so deep and lasting and ours so shallow and fickle?

- How is it that she can forgive and never hold a grudge, but I can't get over a wrong?

- Talk about kindness and courtesy! These people exude those things. I wonder why.

- Where did I miss out on mercy? They have so much more compassion and patience than anyone I've ever known.

- I've never seen such integrity. The guy wouldn't think of taking a dime that is not his.

Do you get the message? It is the difference that makes the difference. "Is this vile world a friend to grace, to help me on to God?" Of course not! It works the other way. The church is a friend to grace to get the attention of those who need God desperately.

Which brings us back to the words Jesus spoke from the hillside in Palestine . . . words full of surprise. Isaac Watts asked, "Am I a soldier of the cross?" Jesus described what a soldier of the cross looked like:

- poor in spirit
- mourning
- gentle
- hungry and thirsty for righteousness
- merciful
- pure in heart
- peacemaking

Talk about *different!* "But I thought we lived in a dog-eat-dog world," the world says. "I thought you had to be tough and rugged and selfish to make it. I mean, if you were to live like that, they would turn you into a doormat." It's true–

> Blessed are you when men cast insults at you, and perse-
> cute you, and say all kinds of evil against you falsely, on
> account of Me. Rejoice, and be glad, for your reward in
> heaven is great, for so they persecuted the prophets who
> were before you.   Matthew 5:11-12

Because your life is a *rebuke* to those who are lost in the swamp of the system, they will put you to the test.

THE ONLY STRATEGY THAT WORKS
IN THE REAL WORLD

Jesus offered the only strategy that would counter-act the world system:

> You are the salt of the earth; but if the salt has become
> tasteless, how will it be made salty again? It is good for
> nothing anymore, except to be thrown out and trampled
> under foot by men. You are the light of the world. A city
> set on a hill cannot be hidden. Nor do men light a lamp,
> and put it under the peck-measure, but on the lampstand;
> and it gives light to all who are in the house. Let your
> light shine before men in such a way that they may see
> your good works, and glorify your Father who is in
> heaven.   Matthew 5:13-16

How in the world can soldiers armed with humility and contrition, gentleness and righteousness, mercy, purity, and peace ever make a lasting impact in a world that is so angry? The answer is found in the words you just read: by shaking salt and shining light. I repeat, to make a lasting impact on the world's system, one must be distinct from it, not identical to it. Jesus puts it so simply: "You are the salt of the earth. . . . You are the light of the world." Not just salt for your neighborhood or for the city where you live. There is enough salt to salt the whole world! Not just a local street light, but enough light to light the entire earth! Incredible statements. And so simple. But don't miss that emphatic "you" in both statements: "*You* are the salt of the earth. *You* are the light of the world."

I don't know if you have been to a basketball game lately, but nowadays one of the popular responses of many fans when a person fouls at a critical moment is to point and shout, "you, you, YOU, YOU! YOU!!" The same applies to one of the referees when he makes a questionable call: "You, You, You, You! YOU!!"

Perhaps we need to move that chant out of the sports arena and into the arena of life. YOU, You, You, You! YOU!! are the light of the world. YOU, You, You, YOU! are the salt of the earth. Nobody else. You're on the spot; you're at the free throw line. Not somebody who has been to seminary. You. Not one of the ordained. You, YOU! All you who know the Savior. Every one of us in God's forever family is to be shaking salt and shining light.

Let's go further. It doesn't say, "You *can* be the salt," or "You *should* be the light." It says, "You *are.*" You don't even need to pray, "Lord, make me real salty. Lord, make me a bright light." You already are. Meaning what? Meaning, get at it. Shake the salt! Shine the light! Simple though it may seem, that is the game plan God has set up for counteracting a world that "lies in the lap of the evil one."

Slowly but surely our world is rotting from within. Not only are civilizations in the process of decaying, but morals are, as well. If Rip Van Winkle were still sleeping and awoke from his nap today, he would be shocked at the eroding standards of our time. What our culture accepts as the norm would have been considered scandalous back when he went to sleep.

The deadly erosion has plunged our world into frighteningly deep darkness. Some Christians have distanced themselves so far from the lifestyle of the unbeliever that they don't have a clue how dark the world system really is. They don't see its boredom, its flat tastelessness, its terror, and its stark hopelessness. There is the inescapable threat of AIDS, along with the abduction of children, alcoholism, and fears of growing old, of financial reversal, of marital infidelity, of emotional breakdown. Such darkness surfaces only briefly, then runs and hides its face in the valley of death.

One morning when I had a few extra minutes, I thumbed through a few pages of a local newspaper. Immediately I felt the edges of darkness closing in:

- A freeway shooter left a driver crippled, paralyzed from the neck down after he was shot in the neck. The gunman was sentenced to a maximum of ten years as the fellow in the wheelchair sat in the back of the courtroom and shook his head in amazement.

- In nearby Santa Ana a man was stabbed to death by two of his "friends."

- A wife and mother shot her daughter, then her husband, and then killed herself. All that happened in a quiet little home a few blocks south of where I live.

- Two men who swindled $9.5 million from several thousand people in telephone scams were sentenced to fifteen to twenty years.

- A wife was found guilty of killing her husband for insurance money.

- A restaurateur was convicted of arson conspiracy in the case of a fire in a neighboring community.

- Jurors convicted an El Toro man of manslaughter.

- During a hotel party, a man fell eight stories,

but was not killed. His fall was broken when he struck a wooden lattice over a bar on the first floor. He was drunk.

- Twenty-two motorists were arrested in one day at checkpoints. All failed the sobriety test.

And all this didn't quite get me halfway through section [2] . . . but I had read enough!

Do you have any idea what that kind of news does to the average citizen? If it doesn't scare the life out of him, it can make him strangely apathetic. Then he gets hardened to it . . . shrugs it off, and says, "Who gives a rip?" So it goes in the darkness. But Jesus has devised a strategy that works.

A Better Taste of the Salt

> You are the salt of the earth; but if the salt has become tasteless, how will it be made salty again? It is good for nothing anymore, except to be thrown out and trampled under foot by men.   Matthew 5:13

Before refrigeration, salt served a vital purpose. Fishermen, for example, knew its value. As soon as they got their catch, they packed the fish in layers of salt to preserve the meat until they could get it to market. Our forefathers who crossed the rugged plains and mountains in prairie schooners often layered their meat in salt or carried meat that had been soaked in brine to preserve it for as long as possible. Salt has a preserving effect. In other words, it arrests corruption.

Salt also adds flavor to food. Just a little shake of salt can dramatically change the taste of a dish. One of salt's most valuable contributions is the "bite" it adds to food. However, it can lose that bite.

I remember a course I took in chemistry in which I learned that sodium chloride is a very stable and resilient chemical compound. In reality, it never becomes "unsalty." Yet Jesus said that salt can become "tasteless." What did He mean? When salt becomes contaminated by dirt, sand, and other impurities, Jesus said it becomes "good for nothing." (Today if somebody is shiftless or lazy or does a poor job, we say that person is "good for nothing." That saying comes from Jesus' words.)

Look at a Christian who has absorbed the world system, and you will see salt that has lost its flavor—a tasteless, useless seasoning. The worse our world becomes, the greater is its need of salt because that's another important property: salt makes you thirsty. In the case of the salty Christian, it makes the surrounding world thirsty for the very water of life. And, by the way, I'm not just talking about huge piles of salt (like big churches and evangelistic crusades) that make folks thirsty for the things of God. I'm talking about consistent, everyday, lifestyle things.

Earl Palmer, in a fine little book entitled *The Enormous Exception,* tells the story of a premed student at the University of California, Berkeley "who became a Christian after a long journey through doubts and questions." When Palmer asked the young man why he had chosen Jesus Christ, he answered that what had "tipped the scales" in his spiritual journey were the actions of a classmate who happened to be a Christian.

During the previous term the premed student had been very ill with the flu and, as a result, had missed ten days of school. "Without any fanfare or complaints," his Christian classmate carefully collected all his class assignments and took time away from his own studies to help him catch up.

The premed student told Palmer, "You know, this kind of thing just isn't done. I wanted to know what made this guy act the way he did. I even found myself asking if I could go to church with him."

God had used a salt-and-light Christian to tip the spiritual scales in this young premed student's life, and the Christian student proved to be a preservative influence "so that in that practical and what might appear quite small series of events his friend and fellow student had been able to find the way to an even more profound preservation of life."

Palmer says,

I think the best tribute I ever heard concerning a Christian was the tribute spoken of this student. "I felt more alive when I was around this friend." It is this life that the disciples felt when they were near Jesus and it is what the world still feels when its people are near to those who know Jesus.[2]

Think about it: Do people feel more alive when they're around you? Do you create a thirst as you "shake the salt"? Does anyone ever wonder why you are so unselfish, so thoughtful, so caring? Do the neighborhood children want to be in your home because of the way you treat your children? And how about the teenagers? Is there some kind of "salty magnet" that draws them toward you?

People who live in darkness not only need salt, they also need light.

A Closer Look at the Light

What is the purpose of light? The answer is not complicated. Light dispels darkness.

Have you ever experienced complete, utter darkness? I vividly remember a couple of times when I have been in unbelievably thick darkness. The first time was when my family visited Carlsbad Caverns in New Mexico. It was in the early 1950s, back in the days when guides would lead groups far down into the bowels of the cavern. I can still remember how they turned off all the lights, and for some reason played a recording of a choir singing "Rock of Ages, Cleft for Me." As a teenager I was more concerned about getting the lights back on than singing along with some choir. It was *so* dark! When I put my hand in front of my face, just a few inches away from the end of my nose, I could feel the heat from my hand, but I could not even make out its silhouette. The cavern was absolutely *inky* black. Then someone struck a match—just one tiny match—and the light shown like a brilliant beacon.

I recall another scene. As a little boy I went flounder fishing along the Texas gulf shores with my father. If you have never floundered, you have missed half the fun of growing up. About the time it starts getting dark, you light a portable lantern and walk down to the edge of the bay; then you wade in until you're about knee deep. Next, you begin to walk very slowly, following the shoreline. By late evening the water has become calm, and the flounders (you hope) have come in close to shore. Using their wide fins, they settle down into the mud and sand and lie there with their mouths wide open, waiting for supper (some unassuming mullet or shrimp dancing in the shallows near the shoreline). What the flounder does not know is that it's going to be someone else's supper! Walking along, swinging the lantern, you peer into the water for the outline of a flounder lying absolutely still. When you spot one, down goes the gig, and, after a flurry of activity, you manage to get it onto your stringer.

Now when I was very small, I was much more concerned about getting back home in the dark than I was about locating flounder on the ocean floor. But I wanted to be with my dad, so I took the risk. If I asked him once, I must have asked him a dozen times, every time we went floundering, "Dad, in case the lantern goes out, do you know how to get back home?"

"Yeah, son. Don't worry . . . we'll get back. No problem. Just watch for the flounder."

"I know, Dad, but is there plenty of fuel in the lantern?"

"Yes, there's plenty of fuel. Now, watch for the flounder."

When we got to one point along the winding shoreline, we could no longer see our bay cottage—that was the point of no return in my little mind. I always feared that transitional moment. I can still remember rounding the point and craning my neck for one last look at the cottage light, because from then on the lantern's glow was our only hope of piercing the darkness.

On one occasion we had gotten a mile or so beyond that point when my dad gigged a flounder. Its fins and wide tail splashed the water up out of the bay in a furious explosion of water and sand.

As the cold water hit the scorching-hot lantern glass—BOOM!—the light went out. It was suddenly pitch black! And I was scared spitless. My dad hadn't told me, but he always carried a flashlight in his hip pocket. What a relief when he snapped it on. I remember asking him, "Are the batteries in the flashlight good?" He reassured me they were new. There we were, miles from home, knee deep in water, and surrounded by thick darkness on a moonless night. That single ray of light was our only hope . . . but it was all we needed.

When you live in the darkness, you not only have no ray of light, you don't even know where home is. That is the way it is for the majority in the world. Some folks are born, raised, and die in cultures that have never seen their first flashlight of hope. Imagine it!

When the truth of that hits me, I find myself a little impatient with Christians who do nothing but shine lights for themselves. They even have what we might call flashlight parties where they just shine the light on each other. Lots of light! Too much light to be hoarded! Jesus says to shine for the world. Shine your light into the darkness; that's where it is really needed. Spend less time in your own little well-lighted all-Christian world and more time there in the darkness!

Years ago I came to appreciate this verse by C. T. Studd:

> Some wish to live within the sound
> Of Church or Chapel bell;
> I want to run a Rescue Shop
> Within a yard of hell.[3]

You say your environment is dark? What an opportunity! You're the only one in the company who knows the Savior? Now you're talking! You've got the light! Now be careful . . . don't shine a big blinding beacon right into your co-worker's eyes. He needs light, but just enough in the right places. And salt? Don't dump a truckload on him. Just a little, please. Too much salt ruins the food just as too much light blinds the eyes.

The counterstrategy is simple: Shake, don't pour. Shine, don't blind.

Remember how Jesus put it? "A city set on a hill cannot be hidden." You couldn't hide it if you tried. Your light is on the hill. "Good works" sound a clarion call. Just live a different life. That will drive them nuts, wondering why *you* don't do the things they do. They won't know why you have peace of mind. They won't know why you don't worry. They won't know why you smile more than you frown. But they'll sure be curious.

It is amazing how light attracts. When you're in a dark place with just one light, all eyes focus on the light. Light is what gives mariners a course to follow across the seas. They determine their direction by the stars, light-years away. The gleam of a lighthouse on the horizon gives a direction. It attracts attention.

"Don't make it complicated," says Jesus. "Simply let your light shine." Isn't that easy? Just let it shine. No need to add extra voltage. No need to make a giant public announcement, proclaiming "I walk in the light." Just shine.

Jesus never said to His disciples, "You know, fellas, we have to work on gathering a better crowd. They're getting pretty thin, especially on Sunday night." No, it was never like that. He just turned on the light and they came to Him. In the wilderness. Or in the city. On a hillside. At the lakeside. They came! He was so different! He was light. And so are we.

What will they see? They will see "your good

works," Jesus said. Like what? They will hear your courtesy. They will detect your smile. They will notice that you stop to thank them. They will hear you apologize when you are wrong. They will see you help them when they are struggling. They will notice that you are the one who stopped along the road and gave them a hand. They will see every visible manifestation of Christ's life being normally lived out through you. They will see all that and they "will glorify your Father who is in heaven" (Matt. 5:16). John R. W. Stott writes:

> I sometimes think how splendid it would be if non-Christians, curious to discover the secret and source of our light, were to come up to us and enquire:

> > Twinkle, twinkle, little star,
> > How I wonder what you are![4]

Isn't it a pleasure when someone says to you, "Why are you like that?" And isn't it a natural thing to respond, "I'm glad you asked. Let me tell you what's happened"? And then you light their way home.

I love the way one man expressed much of what I've been describing in a profound prayer. Profound, yet simple:

> LORD, HIGH AND HOLY, MEEK AND LOWLY,
> Thou hast brought me to the valley of vision,
> where I live in the depths but see thee in the heights;
> hemmed in by mountains of sin I behold thy glory.
> Let me learn by paradox

that the way down is the way up,
that to be low is to be high,
that the broken heart is the healed heart,
that the contrite spirit is the rejoicing spirit,
that the repenting soul is the victorious soul,
that to have nothing is to possess all,
that to bear the cross is to wear the crown,
that to give is to receive,
that the valley is the place of vision.
Lord, in the daytime stars can be seen from deepest
wells,
and the deeper the wells the brighter thy stars shine;
Let me find thy light in my darkness,
thy life in my death,
thy joy in my sorrow,
thy grace in my sin,
thy riches in my poverty,
thy glory in my valley.[5]

SIMPLY PUT: SUGGESTIONS FOR SHAKING AND SHINING

When you shake and shine, you *influence* others, which Webster defines as "the act or power of producing an effect without apparent exertion of force or direct exercise of command."

As one writer says,

We who are married do not have to pretend we are living as Barbie Dolls on a wedding cake. We have struggles, and dashed expectations too. But if we offer the world a model of a reasonably good marriage, a reasonably good church, a reasonably good college fellowship, it will have radicalizing effects on the world.[6]

As I close this chapter, let me mention three "don'ts." First: *Don't overdo it.* Remember, don't call attention to the salt or the light, just live the life. If you are married, perhaps your best testimony in this dark world is little more than "a reasonably good marriage." Isn't that relieving? No need to walk on water.

Second: *Don't hold back.* When you live the life of faith fairly consistently, you will attract the attention of those in the darkness; you will cultivate a thirst in those who are living tasteless, hopeless lives. And when they come asking for information, you will have a perfect opportunity to tell them about the Source of the salt and light.

Take a risk. Take a risk with good works. They will make a difference in this "vile world."

Just consider a few of the specific ways that shake-and-shine Christians have made a difference in the world: abolition of slavery, prison reform, medical care, helping the addicts, world missions, alternatives to abortion, exposing child abuse, establishing orphanages, making a positive influence in the political world, holding leadership positions in large companies that are making an impact in this world—and much more.

Third: ***Don't worry about the few who resist it.***

Nobody bats a thousand. Some even walked away from the Master Himself. (Remember, He was the only perfect human being who ever lived, yet they crucified Him.) Even the great prophets and apostles were ignored, forgotten, and martyred. Don't worry about the few who reject the salt and resist the light.

"Is this vile world a friend to grace, to help me on to God?" In no way. Quite the reverse, in fact. People who are salt and light are the friends of grace. We are the ones who help the world on to God. What a counterstrategy! Best of all, it is simple. Just shake and shine.

CHAPTER FOUR

Simplicity Starts from Within

SOME BIBLICAL scenes would be absolutely great on a videocassette. Not the Cecil B. DeMille productions with all their phony costumes, lavish makeup, special effects, and plastic landscapes. I'm talking about the real thing—the original events—being captured on film for all to see.

How about that time when all those Hebrews crossed the Red Sea? Or when Elijah mocked the prophets of Baal, then called down fire from heaven? I would love to see that moment in Joseph's life when he was surrounded by his brothers and they didn't have a clue that he was their relative . . . and then he revealed his identity. What an ending! Another winner would be Noah's ark—from the inside: wall-to-wall animals cooped up together for weeks in that floating zoo. My long-time mentor and friend, Howie Hendricks, once commented that Noah's family in the ark reminded him of God's family in the church: "If it weren't for all the trouble on the outside, we couldn't stand the stench on the inside."

I suppose each one of us would have our favorite biblical film clips. Being a preacher, I can think of several original "preacher scenes" I would find extremely interesting—like when the prophet Jeremiah wept through a few sermons he preached, or when Jonah made that first amphibious landing and instantly hightailed it to Nineveh. Or imagine the epic adventure of John the Baptizer roaming the wilderness dressed in camel's hair, eating locusts dipped in honey, and shouting, "Repent, you hypocrites!" Classic moments. Watching Paul as he addressed all those eggheads on Mars Hill in Athens would be another scene worth viewing. The city's philosophical brain trust had just labeled him a "seed picker," then minutes later heard him spontaneously quote from one of their own poets as he spoke of Christ's miraculous resurrection! D. Martyn Lloyd-Jones, while delivering a series on preaching at Westminster Theological Seminary years ago, declared:

> What is preaching? Logic on fire! Eloquent reason! Are these contradictions? Of course they are not. Reason concerning this Truth ought to be mightily eloquent, as you see it in the case of the Apostle Paul and others. It is theology on fire! And a theology which does not take fire, I maintain, is a defective theology; or at least the man's understanding of it is defective. Preaching is theology coming through a man who is on fire.[1]

We still have the fiery words of great preachers of the past, but because we cannot literally hear their voices and actually watch their gestures, we miss much of the fire that originally burned in them and through them.

This is especially true regarding the message Jesus delivered on the mountain outside Jerusalem. Talk about a man on fire; the Master was ablaze! Full of passion and zeal, at the zenith of His human manhood, our Lord used the simplest of words to cut to the heart of the issues that mattered, so much so that His hearers sat spellbound. His theology-on-fire gripped their hearts. If you think His style was mild-mannered and passive, you owe yourself another reading of Matthew 5, 6, and 7. No question, He shook up the troops! And this message was one of the earliest in His ministry. It reminds me of a similar style that characterized George Whitefield, that brilliant, eighteenth-century, Oxford-trained proclaimer of truth. The very first Sunday after his ordination Whitefield preached with such fervor that a complaint was made to the bishop, "asserting that as the result of his sermon fifteen people had become insane."[2] That, friends and neighbors, is theology on fire.

THE AUTHORITY OF THE SCRIPTURES

Were we able today to witness Jesus' message in person, I have no doubt that it would stab us awake. Why do I say that? Because He spoke with authority—the all-powerful, invincible authority of the Scriptures.

Human opinions no longer mattered, not even the longstanding, rigidly enforced pharisaic rules and regulations.

Are we talking about merely making an impression or being persuasive? No. Webster defines *authority* as "the power to influence or command thought, opinion, or behavior." I would use two additional words to describe authority: *convincing force* . . . a force far greater than any human can muster. Jesus' words were "living and active" (Heb. 4:12), eclipsing every man-made code of ethics or moral standard.

Why Is Authority Important?

Remove that standard and humanity is awash in this person's opinion or that culture's tradition or some group's regulations, or, most specifically, in pharisaic legalism. In the final analysis, it was when Jesus had the audacity to question those longstanding traditions that plans for His demise were put in motion. If we had a videocassette of His delivering this sermon and if the camera were panning His audience, we would detect a few astonished faces and, no doubt, a few frowns about the time He said the words recorded in Matthew 5:17: "Do not think that I came to abolish the Law or the Prophets; I did not come to abolish, but to fulfill."

Suddenly, for the first time, He—personally—is brought into focus. During the Beatitudes He spoke in the third person: "Blessed are those who," and "blessed are they." When He talked about shaking salt and shining light, He subtly shifted the pronouns from third to second person: "You are the salt . . . you are the light." But now? Now He speaks of Himself. Why does He do this? Because some must have wondered if He was speaking on His own behalf. Maybe one or two thought, *Who does He think He is? Is He above the Law? Sounds like He sets Himself up as judge and jury. Is He beyond the authority of Scripture?*

THE FULFILLMENT OF THE LAW

Let's not make Jesus' statement complicated. He gave it to simplify the issue, not confuse His hearers.

The Law and Christ

His initial remark stands on its own. He had not come to cancel out the Law or to remove its authority. Then how are we to interpret His second comment? "I did not come to abolish, but to fulfill." In what way?

Think about it. He brought the Scripture to completion in His person. Old Testament Scripture speaks often of the Messiah who was to come. "I am He," implies Jesus. Furthermore, He fulfilled Scripture when He gave it a literal point of reference. Periodically during His earthly ministry Jesus mentioned, "This fulfills what was spoken by the prophet." He also fulfilled Scripture by obeying its moral code and ethical commands. At every point, He obeyed. Never once did He compromise or hedge.

In fact, if you still wonder if Jesus was a little soft on Scripture, get a load of His next statement:

> For truly I say to you, until heaven and earth pass away, not the smallest letter or stroke shall pass away from the Law, until all is accomplished.   Matthew 5:18

I can remember when the only Bible every Christian used was the King James Version. Because it renders this verse a little differently, let me quote it here.

> For verily I say unto you, Till heaven and earth pass, one jot or one tittle shall in no wise pass from the law, till all be fulfilled.

Study those two unusual words, *jot* and *tittle*. What is Jesus saying here? The word *jot* is literally a transliteration of a Hebrew character, *yodh*. It is the smallest letter in the twenty-two characters of the Hebrew alphabet. In the King James Version it is translated "jot"; in the New American Standard translation it is "smallest letter." It is a tiny character that looks a bit like an apostrophe.

But if you think that's tiny, the tittle is even more so. In Hebrew, two letters look almost identical. If it were not for an additional "tail" on the end of one of those letters, you would swear they were the same. In fact, they would be. The only difference is that tiny additional part of the letter. And that very small part of one letter is called the tittle.

It is as if Jesus were saying, "I so believe in the authority and the preservation and the inspiration of Scripture that not even the dot above an *i* or the cross on a *t* shall pass away until it has all been fulfilled." Jesus erased all questions regarding His commitment to Scripture or obedience to its command.

But the truth is, God was still in the process of revealing His truth as He spoke through His Son Jesus. In that process, God wanted His people to know more than the letter of the Law, but in no way were they to erase the truths of the Old Testament or take them lightly, which is why Jesus adds,

> Whoever then annuls one of the least of these commandments, and so teaches others, shall be called least in the kingdom of heaven; but whoever keeps and teaches them, he shall be called great in the kingdom of heaven. Matthew 5:19

The Law and the Christian

What is life in the kingdom of heaven? Generally speaking—simply speaking—it is a life lived under the authority of Scripture. If you take advantage of it, if you compromise it, if you fuss around and say it does not mean what it says or it means something other than what it actually says, you will miss much of what God has in mind for us in kingdom living.

Jesus goes on to say:

> For I say to you, that unless your righteousness surpasses that of the scribes and Pharisees, you shall not enter the kingdom of heaven.   Matthew 5:20

Again, if we had a few video shots of some Pharisees when they heard these words, we would be looking at frowning stares, for sure. No one was more pious in appearance than the Pharisees. They wore certain garments that gave them an externally religious look. They conducted themselves in a publicly pious way. They said words that made them seem so holy and at the same time made others feel guilty. But don't misunderstand. Externally it seemed as though they fulfilled every letter of the Law, but what was missing was the spirit of the Law. Jesus says, in effect, "Unless your righteousness goes deeper than theirs, unless your genuine faith surpasses their external piety, you don't know what kingdom living is all about." It is the inner heart that God searches and rewards.

A quick trip to the animal world might help. You can take a pig out of the pigpen and you can wash that pig until it is spotless. You can then spray it with the finest perfume. You can even put a pink ribbon around its neck and teach it to snort for its food. But as soon as you turn that pig loose and allow it to be itself again, it will go back to the muddy pigsty and dive right into the slop for dinner. Why? Because you have not changed its heart—its "pigness."

Howie Stevenson, my dear friend and minister of worship and music at our church, has this saying framed and hanging on his office wall:

> Never try to teach a pig to sing.
> It wastes your time and it annoys the pig.

The Pharisees were big on external washings; they were good at perfume, great at pink ribbons and all kinds of public tricks, but they missed the heart. They cared little about that.

Jesus wasn't always tactful with the grace-killing Pharisees of His day. A little later in His ministry, as their attacks on Him intensified, He exposed them without mercy.

> You hypocrites, rightly did Isaiah prophesy of you, saying,
>> "This people honors Me with their lips,
>> But their heart is far away from Me.
>> But in vain do they worship Me,
>> Teaching as doctrines the precepts
>> of men."   Matthew 15:7-9

Then in order to encourage His followers to live authentic rather than hypocritical lives, Jesus immediately called them aside and warned, "Not what enters into the mouth defiles the man, but what proceeds out of the mouth, this defiles the man" (Matt. 15:11).

Wow! That hit home, too. For the Pharisees not only talked about washing, they were very big on diet. The Jews had to eat certain foods a certain way or they broke the traditions. Now Jesus was saying, "It doesn't matter that much what goes into the mouth. What really matters is what comes out."

I love the next verse. It always makes me smile: "Then the disciples came and said to Him, 'Do You know that the Pharisees were offended when they heard this statement?'" (Matt. 15:12).

So? Big deal! They *needed* to be offended. One might hope the well-deserved rebuke would awaken them. Unfortunately it didn't, not even when Jesus dug deeper.

> Let them alone; they are blind guides of the blind. And if a blind man guides a blind man, both will fall into a pit. . . .
>
> Do you not understand that everything that goes into the mouth passes into the stomach, and is eliminated? But the things that proceed out of the mouth come from the heart, and those defile the man. For out of the heart come evil thoughts, murders, adulteries, fornications, thefts, false witness, slanders. These are the things which defile the man; but to eat with unwashed hands does not defile the man.   Matthew 15:14, 17-20

I think the point is as simple as it is obvious: In the final analysis, what is significant is that which comes out of the heart. The Pharisees never got the message. Simply put, their faith had lost its simplicity.

The Law and Righteousness

Up to this moment, Jesus' message has been fairly general. From now on, however, He gets quite specific; in fact, He addresses six areas where what goes on in the heart is more important than what occurs on the surface.

To clarify what is coming, let me offer a simple overview. In each of the six popular topics He mentions in this section of Matthew 5, Jesus offers quotes either from the Law or from the traditional teachings of the day; then with each one He gives insight on how to model a righteousness that surpasses all the external stuff.

Subject	*Traditional Teaching New Insight*
Murder (vv. 21–26)	"You have heard" "but I say"
Adultery (vv. 27–30)	"You have heard" "but I say"
Divorce (vv. 31–32)	"It was said" "but I say"
Oaths (vv. 33–37)	"You have heard" "but I say"

Retaliation (vv. 38–42)	"You have heard"
	"but I say"
Love (vv. 43–47)	"You have heard"
	"but I say"

No one can ever accuse Jesus of overlooking or dodging relevant issues. The list remains up-to-date, even though it is over nineteen centuries old. We shall consider only the first subject in the remainder of this chapter, then we will look at the other five later on.

First,

> You have heard that the ancients were told, "You shall not commit murder" and "Whoever commits murder shall be liable to the court."   Matthew 5:21

Jesus begins the list of six issues by mentioning both the Mosaic Law ("the ancients") and the civil law ("the court") regarding murder. It is homicide He has in mind, a premeditated taking of another life, and the Law specifically condemned such: "You shall not commit murder." As time passed, "Whoever commits murder shall be liable to the court" was added. His listeners were especially familiar with that, since the Pharisees taught that rule almost to the exclusion of the initial commandment.

Because Jesus was urging them to attain a righteousness surpassing that of the Pharisees, He goes deeper than the surface—He goes to the heart with the words:

> You have heard that the ancients were told, "You SHALL NOT COMMIT MURDER" and "Whoever commits murder shall be liable to the court." But I say to you that everyone who is angry with his brother shall be guilty before the court; and whoever shall say to his brother, "Raca," shall be guilty before the supreme court; and whoever shall say, "You fool," shall be guilty enough to go into the fiery hell.   Matthew 5:21-22

All right, let's wade into that statement. Clearly, Jesus is describing an anger that goes beyond proper bounds. Let me clarify this, because some will think Jesus is teaching that we should never express anger at all. But if that were the case, God would have been guilty of breaking His own command (remember reading about "the wrath of God"?). In fact, later on in the New Testament Paul teaches in Ephesians 4:26, "BE ANGRY, AND YET DO NOT SIN." So there is a place for appropriate anger. There is justified anger. But Jesus is not referring to that here in His sermon.

Go back and read verse 22 again. Occasionally in a musical score you will find a crescendo symbol. This verse is like that . . . the anger is seen as a crescendo that builds through three stages to the point of murderous statements and thoughts. To begin with there is anger at its basic level, "everyone who is angry with his brother."

Then comes the second stage: "whoever shall say to his brother, 'Raca.'" *Raca* is an Aramaic term that means "empty," most often used with reference to mental emptiness. Our colloquialism today might be "airhead," "nitwit," "bonehead," "numbskull," or "blockhead," any one of those slang expressions. It is an insulting term used in anger against a person. In other words, if someone gets so angry with another that he looks at him and either thinks, says, or shouts, "You mentally worthless idiot!" he or she has gone too far.

Finally Jesus moves to stage three: "and whoever shall say, 'You fool.'" In the original Greek the word is *moros*. Can you guess which term we get from that? Yes, of course: *moron*. It was used most often with reference to people who lived morally wasted lives. In other words, by calling someone this you take the position of a judge because you have determined that that person is morally wasted. And what happens? You "shall be guilty enough to go into the fiery hell." Be careful here. Do not put words into Jesus' mouth. He does not say you go to hell; He says it brings *enough* guilt to send one to hell. This third stage is verbal murder . . . long-lived, nursed anger that is sustained to a vicious point. It bursts out of the mouth in a rage. Remember, the tongue speaks from the heart. And in this case the heart has entertained degrading and insulting thoughts of contempt.

Anger can be difficult to control, and sometimes we fail. But when we get to stage three, we've gone too far. It is nothing less than a verbal stabbing from the heart. It murders the other person with a sharp, knifelike insult. Yet we will allow ourselves to get so completely out of control that we don't even think twice. In fact, we rationalize that, "she had it coming," or "he deserved to hear that." Whoa! If you and I are kingdom people, we don't let that happen.

Jesus mentions two examples that were probably imaginary cases. It is doubtful He had someone specific in mind, but they were certainly true to life. One took place at the temple and the other occurred in the courts. One is in a religious setting and the other in a legal setting. In verses 23 and 24 we have the religious scene, and in verses 25 and 26, the legal scene.

> If therefore you are presenting your offering at the altar, and there remember that your brother has something against you, leave your offering there before the altar, and go your way; first be reconciled to your brother, and then come and present your offering.   Matthew 5:23–24

This is one of the few times in the Bible when we are instructed to interrupt our worship with something that is even more important.

The scenario might go something like this. You get up early Sunday morning and get ready, drive to church, locate a parking spot, and make your way inside. You sit down and begin to prepare yourself for worship. In doing so, you start to focus on the Lord. Beautiful music surrounds you as the organist begins to play some quiet strains of familiar hymns. People around you are talking about things that are joyful and encouraging. It is a peaceful scene, perhaps different from where you work or what you live with. Soon you begin to commune with your Lord. You start to pray. But your eyes haven't been closed sixty seconds when, suddenly, flashing across the back of your eyelids is a face or a name—not just any face, but an individual you offended. You remember it well. The Lord brings that person to your attention. He pulls up that face on your memory screen, and He won't let you forget it. You try to ignore the promptings . . . to go on in worship . . . to sing the words of the hymns; but you are blocked. The Lord is saying, in so many words, "You have to make that right." Maybe it's a former business associate, maybe your marriage partner. Maybe it's your ex. Maybe it's somebody on your ball team that you took advantage of recently, or somebody who is furious with you at school, or an angry neighbor. You are clear about one thing: There is an offense. And what eats your heart out is he knows or she knows that you are the offender. So? Jesus says to "leave your offering there." To apply it literally, you excuse yourself, get up from the pew, walk out the door, get in your car, and drive away. You get in touch with that offended person.

Jesus doesn't say, "Wait a week and pray about it, then write a letter or make a quick phone call." He says, "Go and be reconciled first." That's an order.

Your goal is to turn enmity into amity. You have offended someone. This is not a passing offense or slight thing; it is a heavy weight on your mind. It won't leave you alone because you know the offense has not been reconciled. The best thing to do? Keep it simple–go and make it right.

This is a book on simple faith, and here is another example of how many people complicate their lives instead of simplifying them. You've done wrong? You've been offensive? Your actions or words have caused hurt? To do nothing is not only in direct disobedience to Jesus' teaching, it also complicates your life. It adds heavier mental weights than you are capable of carrying. It is like dropping an anchor and then cranking up your boat's engine and putting it in gear. The anchor keeps catching and snagging on the bottom, making for a terribly uncomfortable ride across the water. How simple the solution! Just pull in the anchor. (By the way, I've never been on a boat with an automatic return anchor. If you dropped it out . . . you need to pull it in.)

Are you nursing a lingering offense? That is, does someone have a lingering offense against you? Let me give you a simple tip: We cannot be right with God until we are right with others. That is the whole gist of this statement.

Here's another one. You might say, "Well, it's true I've had a problem with that guy, but, you know, he's not a Christian. He's more like an enemy, an opponent." Well, I'm glad you brought him up. Jesus adds this counsel regarding our opponents:

> Make friends quickly with your opponent at law while you
> are with him on the way, in order that your opponent may
> not deliver you to the judge, and the judge to the officer,
> and you be thrown into prison.   Matthew 5:25

In other words, solve the problem before it gets to court—before it really gets serious.

Do you like defending your rights? Are you the type of person who always has an attorney ready to help you get your way? If you're not, you are unusual. As I mentioned earlier in this volume, this is the day for threatening each other with lawsuits. I've met folks who sit anxiously on the edge of their seats, just waiting for a chance to sue. Jesus' words stand squarely against that attitude. You want to be different? Jesus suggests, "Solve it out of court."

Simplicity starts from within. Is there so much pride in your heart that you are going to get your way, no matter what? That is nothing but anger, pure and simple, that has gotten out of control—which takes us back to the whole issue of murder. Jesus is concerned about estranged feelings that grow into a small sore. Then the sore festers, comes to a head, and fills with pus; then it bursts, with corruption oozing all over the relationship. The simple (not easy, mind you, *simple*) answer is to work it out between you. Jesus spoke with fire in His bones. We cannot be right with God until we are right with one another.

SIMPLY PUT: THE RELEVANCE
OF THE TRUTH

As I reflect on these wonderful words of life, I find three principles worth pondering.

First: *The principles of Scripture go deeper than externals.* The Pharisees never learned this. If all you get from your church or from your Bible study is surface religion and the importance of superficial appearance, you are missing what true Christianity is all about. If your heart is not being convicted and moved to change, there is something missing that is terribly important. There are unspoken motives that must be addressed. There are personal secrets that await your attention, perhaps a hidden agenda that you have not yet acknowledged. The authoritative Scripture penetrates far below the surface.

Second: *The potential of anger is greater than words.* You can be a killer yet never hold a lethal weapon in your hand. Don't ignore the murder in your attitude.

You may live in an argumentative family. You may have developed the habits of answering back, being defensive, sarcastic, caustic. You may have a violent temper. You are missing the best of kingdom living by letting that linger. Come to terms with those habits. Once you do, you will be amazed how much it will simplify your life.

Third: *The power of reconciliation is stronger than revenge.* It is amazing how forgiveness unloads the weapon in the other person's hand. When you reconcile with your brother or sister, it is amazing what it does in both hearts. It is like having your nervous system flushed out. It is like getting over a longstanding fever and cleansing the corruption that has been diseasing your mind. You don't need an attorney for that. You probably don't need a minister or a counselor, either. You just need humility. To put it straight, in the final analysis you need *guts*. Don't wait any longer . . . draw in the anchor.

It was said that in ancient days Saint Patrick, one of the early saints, had this prayer inscribed on his breastplate:

> God be in my head,
>   And in my understanding;
> God be in my eyes,
>   And in my looking;
> God be in my mouth,
>   And in my speaking;
> God be in my heart,
>   And in my thinking;
> God be at mine end,
>   And at my departing.[3]

Simplicity starts from within. Start!

CHAPTER FIVE

Simple Instructions on Serious Issues

IT IS EASY for those who speak in public to substitute length for strength. There is this mistaken idea that a talk needs to be long before folks will think it's important. Ministers are the most notorious when it comes to this strange logic. Somehow we feel the longer the sermon the more memorable its contents when, in fact, others know better.

One Sunday afternoon a preacher asked his wife, "Do you think I put enough fire in my sermon?" She answered, "To tell the truth, I didn't think you put enough of your sermon into the fire!"

If cleanliness is next to godliness in a home, brevity and clarity are next to accuracy in a sermon. Truth spoken to the point sticks, and anyone who makes a living with his or her voice will testify that preparing a short message is a much greater challenge than a long one. You really have to have a clear picture of what you want to say.

A sculptor was once asked by a group of visitors how he carved such a realistic lion when he didn't have a model. His response brought smiles, though he wasn't trying to amuse them: "I simply carve away anything that doesn't look like a lion."

Jesus was the best when it came to communication. He knew precisely what He wanted to say and how to say it so anyone could understand it. He was often criticized for *what* He said but *never* for how long it took Him to say it. He never wasted a word. Before long, people realized that, from start to finish, His words were worth their undivided attention. Paul O'Neil, a writer for *Life* magazine for many years, would surely have given Jesus an A for His ability to model "O'Neil's Law" to perfection: "Always grab the reader by the throat in the first paragraph, sink your thumbs into his windpipe in the second and hold him against the wall until the tag line."[1] Sounds so easy . . . until you try to do it.

A BRIEF REMINDER OF THE SERMON'S BEGINNING

Jesus didn't merely try to do it in His Sermon on the Mount, He did it. No message has ever distilled more truth in fewer words. In less than twenty minutes He left his audience reeling . . . thoroughly convinced. To this day great minds are still impressed with that command performance delivered on an ancient hill-

side. James T. Fisher, a seasoned psychiatrist, was correct in his observation:

> If you were to take the sum total of all the authoritative
> articles ever written by the most qualified of psycholo-
> gists and psychiatrists on the subject of mental hygiene–
> if you were to combine them and define them and cleave
> out the excess verbiage–if you were to take the whole of
> the meat and none of the parsley, and if you were to have
> these unadulterated bits of pure scientific knowledge
> concisely expressed by the most capable of living poets,
> you would have an awkward and incomplete summation
> of the Sermon on the Mount.[2]

Blessings, Blessings!

Talk about coming to the point! Jesus bypassed all
clichés and predictable preliminaries as He began His
message. He didn't even say, "It's nice to be with you
today." Like a fleet sprinter leaping from his starting
blocks, Jesus offered a quick series of back-to-back
blessings.

- Blessed are the poor in spirit . . .

- Blessed are those who mourn . . .

- Blessed are the gentle . . .

- Blessed are those who hunger and thirst for
  righteousness . . .

- Blessed are the merciful . . .

- Blessed are the pure in heart . . .

- Blessed are the peacemakers . . .

- Blessed are those who have been persecuted . . .

His opening words grabbed everyone by the throat. Full
attention was riveted on the Nazarene from that moment on.

Shake and Shine!

Next, He challenged His listeners to make a difference. How? "You are the salt. . . . You are the
light, . . ."–single-syllable, easily understandable
terms, familiar to everyone. The exhortation fit the
symbols to perfection: "Since you are salt, shake it!
Since you are light, shine!" In other words, "Be different!"

Watch Your Attitude!

After challenging them to demonstrate a righteousness that surpassed that of the scribes and Pharisees,
He got specific. In fact, He dug beneath the surface of
inappropriate actions and addressed two deep-seated
attitudes.

Surface Action	Deeper Attitude
Murder (v. 5:21)	Unrestrained anger (v. 5:22)
Unresolved conflict (v. 5:23)	Lack of forgiveness (vv. 5:24–26)

Then, as we shall soon discover, He goes on to deal with two more realms of righteousness that were ignored and rationalized by the religious teachers of that day: marital fidelity (vv. 27–32) and verbal integrity (vv. 33–37). Some preachers, then and now, avoid sticky issues as though they are sidestepping puddles of hot tar. Not Jesus. With a beautiful blend of courage, wisdom, and simplicity, He waded right in.

A CLEAR DECLARATION OF TWO ABSOLUTES

I find it nothing short of amazing that the subjects Christ addressed in His century-one sermon are as relevant today as they were when He first spoke. Murder and conflicts. Divorce and lies. We've considered the first two; let's hear Him on the next two.

Marital Fidelity

You have heard that it was said, "YOU SHALL NOT COMMIT ADULTERY"; but I say to you, that everyone who looks on a woman to lust for her has committed adultery with her already in his heart. And if your right eye makes you stumble, tear it out, and throw it from you; for it is better for you that one of the parts of your body perish, than for your whole body to be thrown into hell. And if your right hand makes you stumble, cut it off, and throw it from you; for it is better for you that one of the parts of your body perish, than for your whole body to go into hell. And it was said, "WHOEVER SENDS HIS WIFE AWAY, LET HIM GIVE HER A CERTIFICATE OF DIVORCE"; but I say to you that everyone who divorces his wife, except for the cause of unchastity, makes her commit adultery; and whoever marries a divorced woman commits adultery."

Matthew 5:27–32

He begins by quoting the sixth commandment, which everyone in His audience knew painfully well. From childhood, all Jewish citizens had had the commandments drilled into their heads. With consistency, every synagogue service reminded the congregation of that moral code Moses brought down from Mount Sinai: No adultery! But Jesus goes further. Jewish ears all over that hillside must have perked up when He added, "But I say to you. . . ." Why go further? What more needed to be said? Surely "Do not commit adultery" was sufficient, right? Not if we are going to the heart of the problem . . . not if the goal is a righteousness that surpasses pharisaic righteousness.

Jesus never promoted a performance-oriented, surface-only religious lifestyle, but rather an authentic, true-to-the-core life of faith. So if that's true, then the subject of adultery must be traced to the origin of the problem: the inner person where thoughts find their root. To put it straight, long before adultery takes place in the bed, it has already been visualized in the head. Therefore, Jesus added, "but I say to you, that everyone who looks on a woman to lust for her has committed adultery with her already in his heart" (Matt. 5:28).

Those words are familiar to us today, but back then? Revolutionary. Absolutely and shockingly revolutionary. By going to the heart of the issue, Jesus' simplified instructions removed the gray areas related to adultery. He introduced an unheard-of equation: unbridled lust equals adultery.

Some have taken His subsequent words about tearing out an eye or cutting off a hand literally. With great zeal and little wisdom they have followed His words to the letter. Origen of Alexandria actually made himself a eunuch. In A.D. 325 at the Council of Nicea, self-mutilation was finally declared a barbarous practice and officially forbidden.

But Jesus said of the eye that makes us stumble, "tear it out." Should we take Him literally? I think not . . . otherwise, every man I know would be blind! On this issue of interpreting such Scriptures literally, I am often reminded of C. S. Lewis's words:

> There is no need to be worried by facetious people who try to make the Christian hope of "Heaven" ridiculous by saying they do not want "to spend eternity playing harps." The answer to such people is that if they cannot understand books written for grown-ups, they should not

talk about them. All the scriptural imagery (harps, crowns, gold, etc.) is, of course, a merely symbolical attempt to express the inexpressible. Musical instruments are mentioned because for many people (not all) music is the thing known in the present life which most strongly suggests ecstasy and infinity. Crowns are mentioned to suggest the fact that those who are united with God in eternity share His splendour and power and joy. Gold is mentioned to suggest the timelessness of Heaven (gold does not rust) and the preciousness of it. People who take these symbols literally might as well think that when Christ told us to be like doves, He meant that we were to lay eggs.[3]

Well, then, how do we make sense of what He taught regarding marital fidelity? It helps me to go back to what our Lord actually said: "everyone who looks on a woman *to lust for her* has committed adultery with her already in his heart" (italics mine). He is not speaking of simply looking at another person, but looking for the purpose of lusting. Such looks obviously pass through the eye gate. Furthermore, lust can be intensified by wrong uses of our hands as well as allowing our feet to take us places where our sexual restraints are weakened. All these actions stimulate seductive and sensual feelings within us (in the "heart"), and when that happens it is as if we have actually acted out illicit expressions of sex.

So? So, do not look to prompt lust. Do not touch to

stimulate lust. In today's terms, do not undress a man or woman in your mind as you stare at the physical appearance. Do not linger at the magazine rack or rent X-rated videos or watch films that stir your sensual desires. And, ladies, you can cooperate by refusing to wear seductive attire. By saying no to such things, you "tear out your eye" and you "cut off your hand." One of the best ways I have found to obey Jesus' instruction is simply to replace sensual thoughts with wholesome ones . . . to occupy my mind with things that are pure, lovely, healthy, and positive rather than lurid, provocative, and questionable. Scripture memory works wonders, frankly. I find it impossible to simultaneously lust and repeat verses on moral purity.

Issue of Divorce

Jesus builds on His words regarding lustful thoughts by turning our attention to divorce.

> And it was said, "WHOEVER SENDS HIS WIFE AWAY, LET HIM GIVE HER A CERTIFICATE OF DIVORCE"; but I say to you that everyone who divorces his wife, except for the cause of unchastity, makes her commit adultery; and whoever marries a divorced woman commits adultery.   Matthew 5:31-32

He begins by quoting words from Moses' pen, written

centuries earlier in the ancient book of Deuteronomy.
Let me quote that original source:

> When a man takes a wife and marries her, and it hap-
> pens that she finds no favor in his eyes because he has
> found some indecency in her, and he writes her a certifi-
> cate of divorce and puts it in her hand and sends her out
> from his house, and she leaves his house and goes and
> becomes another man's wife, and if the latter husband
> turns against her and writes her a certificate of divorce
> and puts it in her hand and sends her out of his house, or
> if the latter husband dies who took her to be his wife, then
> her former husband who sent her away is not allowed to
> take her again to be his wife, since she has been defiled;
> for that is an abomination before the LORD, and you shall
> not bring sin on the land which the LORD your God gives
> you as an inheritance.   Deuteronomy 24:1-4

Originally, when "a certificate of divorce" was first
used, it came as a concession because of the hardness
of the Hebrews' hearts. It was not commanded; it was
permitted, reluctantly and rarely.

It may help you to know that when Jesus spoke of divorce, He addressed a hot issue that was often debated
among religious leaders in His day. Contradictory positions were taught in rival rabbinic schools, Shammai
and Hillel. Rabbi Shammai, the conservative, took a rig-
orous approach. He founded his teaching on
Deuteronomy 24:1, which he felt allowed divorce strictly
on the basis of some grave matrimonial offense or inde-

cent act of unchastity. This austere position grew out of Shammai's extremely strict interpretation of Scripture. Rabbi Hillel, on the other hand, adopted a much more lax position. Josephus, a well-known Jewish historian, states that Hillel applied the Mosaic provision to a man who "desires to be divorced from his wife for any cause whatsoever."[4] We are talking superliberal here. For example, a man could divorce his wife,

- if she spoiled his dinner by adding too much salt,
- if she were seen in public with her head uncovered,
- if she talked with other men on the street,
- if she spoke disrespectfully to her husband's parents,
- if she became plain-looking compared with another woman who seemed more beautiful in her husband's opinion.

Unbelievable! For the most insignificant and subjective reasons imaginable, a first-century divorce was justified by rabbis who had been trained at the Hillel school. This explains why, a little later on, some Pharisees put Jesus to the test by pressing Him on His position regarding divorce:

> And some Pharisees came to Him, testing Him, and saying, "Is it lawful for a man to divorce his wife for any cause at all?"   Matthew 19:3

Apparently they wondered if He agreed with the Hillel school of thought. In other words, "In which camp are you, Jesus, Shammai's or Hillel's?" His answer revealed He was in neither camp. In fact, His whole line of reasoning differed from theirs.

As I examine Jesus' teaching, both in Matthew 19 and here in His sermon on the mountain, I find three contrasts between His position and the Pharisees' position:

1. The Pharisees were preoccupied with grounds for divorce, but Jesus was much more concerned with the *institution of marriage.* They wanted to know how to get free from the commitment, while He emphasized the sanctity and permanence of the partnership.

2. The Pharisees called Moses' provision a command, while Jesus considered it a *concession.* This is not nitpicking at words. The former calls for obedience and seems to justify their desire for divorce. The latter holds much tighter reins on the issue, making divorce a reluctant and hesitant act of regrettable compromise.

3. The Pharisees regarded divorce *lightly.* Jesus always viewed it *seriously.* They were forever on a search for reasons to claim a marriage could end, while Jesus resisted such an attitude. He stood steadfastly for the bond that was sealed at the time of marriage.[5]

I am fully aware of the unhappiness in many marriages. Having served in the pastorate for almost thirty years (and having remained at the same church for over twenty of those years), there are not many stories I haven't heard. While I am certainly not one whose position is so rigid I would never see a reason for divorce, I must express my grave concern over the tragic erosion of marital fidelity I have witnessed during the past three decades. My plea is that couples take their marriage vows far more seriously . . . that they see their vows as a lifelong commitment to one another, "for better or for worse," because there is a lot of both! I realize my conservative position is not news to anyone who knows me well, but if it helps hold even one couple together, it will have been worth my repeating the obvious: Marriage is for life. Let's make it last!

If it will help, return to those initial beatitudes Jesus spoke and apply them to marriage. Remember those blessings our Lord gave to the gentle, the poor in spirit, the merciful, and several other groups of greathearted souls? Chrysostom, that ancient saint, offers this appropriate counsel:

> He that is meek and a peacemaker and poor in spirit and merciful, how shall he cast out his wife? He that is used to reconciling others, how shall he be at variance with her who is his own?[6]

Let's return to Jesus' final comment on marriage in His great sermon:

But I say to you that everyone who divorces his wife, except for the cause of unchastity, makes her commit adultery; and whoever marries a divorced woman commits adultery.   Matthew 5:32

The exception clause that appears in Jesus' statement here is probably the most popular exception clause in all the Scriptures, "except for unchastity." There is no need to complicate the issue. Simplicity, remember, is His style. I take it to mean what it says: that divorce may occur when there is sexual intimacy by a married partner with someone outside the marriage bond and it continues to occur as a habit or as a lifestyle. Why? Because that clearly destroys the bond. (This is not the only place where divorce is addressed in Scripture. In case you are wrestling with the subject and want to probe more deeply into the other Scriptures as well, I suggest you read chapter 9 in my book *Strike the Original Match.*)

An unfaithful mate may give you the right to seek divorce, but you are not obligated to exercise that right. Remember, divorce is a God-given concession, not a command. The laws of our land give us the right to sue whomever we wish, but most of us live our entire lives and never sue anyone. Instead, we swallow hard, take it on the chin, and occasionally live with mistreatment. Why? Because taking someone to court, like divorcing an unfaithful mate, is not an obligation, but a concession. Before you yield to a divorce, I suggest one simple exercise, taken seriously: Review what you vowed when you got married.

Verbal Integrity

Speaking of vows, Jesus deals next with verbal honesty.

> Again, you have heard that the ancients were told, "YOU SHALL NOT MAKE FALSE VOWS, BUT SHALL FULFILL YOUR VOWS TO THE LORD." But I say to you, make no oath at all, either by heaven, for it is the throne of God, or by the earth, for it is the footstool of His feet, or by Jerusalem, for it is THE CITY OF THE GREAT KING. Nor shall you make an oath by your head, for you cannot make one hair white or black. But let your statement be, "Yes, yes" or "No, no"; and anything beyond these is of evil.   Matthew 5:33–37

I confess, I read that a dozen times before it began to make sense, so be encouraged if at first glance it seems confusing.

Let's not make it complicated. Obviously, the subject is people who speak the truth. Oaths have to do with taking vows for the purpose of adding veracity to a statement. When I borrow a book from you and say to you, "I'll give it back; I promise," that is a vow. To use the biblical term, it is an oath. Other illustrations come to mind. When our president takes office, he puts his hand on a Bible and makes a vow to uphold the Constitution of the United States of America. We even call that "taking the oath of office." Individuals who are ordained into ministry take vows that relate to being faithful to minister as they commit themselves to a life of purity and devotion to Jesus Christ and His Word. When you go to a courtroom to be a witness, you swear "to tell the truth, the whole truth, and nothing but the truth, so help me God." You make an oath. It doesn't keep you from perjury, but it makes you liable if you commit perjury, because you vowed to tell the truth.

When Jesus says, "Make no oath at all," is He disavowing all oaths? Is He telling our president not to put his hand on a Bible and swear that he will uphold the Constitution? I don't think so. Jesus' comment has to do with vows that are added to a statement, thinking that the additional promises will make the statement trustworthy. They don't. The point is, our word ought to stand. When a monosyllable will do, why waste our breath on polysyllables? Once again, keep it simple. Say yes or say no. Verbosity is no guarantee of veracity.

You say, "That's no big deal. My goodness, anybody could do that." Well, let me probe a little. Let's suppose you promised you would pay off a portion of a debt every month. Are you doing that? To go a step further, are your payments on time? Or let's say you needed a tool, so you borrowed it from your neighbor with the promise that you would return it soon as you were finished. Have you? You promised that you would be true to your mate. Are you? At a serious moment of conviction you promised your Lord you would stand up for Him. Have you been doing that? There's no need to add a lot of additional words or high-sounding oaths of reassurance; just do it.

Some people think that by adding words they will make their statements all the more believable. Not so. All that's needed is, "I'll meet you here tomorrow afternoon at two o'clock," not "I'll meet you here, for sure, tomorrow afternoon at two o'clock. I swear to you, you can count on it. By the authority of heaven, I will keep my word." That doesn't add veracity to the promise. I just need to be sure I am where I said I would be at two o'clock. Yes ought to mean yes. No should mean no. Keep it simple.

Sometimes a simple statement of truth can be a strong motivation for those around you. Korean evangelist Billy Kim tells a wonderful story that beautifully illustrates my point.

After the war the communists swept down into South Korea from the North. One of the first things they did was to gather a group of Christians into their church building, where they demanded that the leaders deny their Lord. They backed up their demands with torture and threats to the lives of their prisoners. One by one the leaders succumbed. When their torturers handed them the Bible and told them to spit upon it, they did so. Until the communists came to one little girl.

Fearlessly she looked at her tormentors and said, "You can hammer me into a pulp. You can beat me into extinction, but I will never deny my Lord!" Then she began to sing, after turning to the leaders who had fallen to say, "May God have mercy on your souls." What was the result? The crowd with her in the church joined her in singing. She turned the tide of denial that had been begun by the leaders. What did the communists do? They executed the leaders who had denied Christ and set free the girl whose courage had been so clearly communicated.[7]

Jesus' counsel is clear: Let your yes be *yes*; let your no be *no.* In other words, be known as a person of verbal integrity. Special and sometimes surprising results await those who refuse to pad the record or add a lot of self-justifying remarks. God honors simple honesty.

In his work, *The Christian Century*, Lloyd Steffen writes of a time back in the eighteenth century when King Frederick II of Prussia visited a Berlin prison. One inmate after another tried to convince the monarch of his innocence. Amazing! To hear them tell it, they were all being unjustly punished for crimes they never committed–all, that is, except one man who sat quietly in a corner while all the rest unfolded their lengthy and complicated stories.

Seeing him sitting there, oblivious to the commotion, the king asked the man why he was in prison. "Armed robbery, Your Honor."

The king asked, "Were you guilty?"

"Yes, sir," he answered, without attempting to excuse his wrongdoing.

King Frederick then gave the guard an order: "Release this guilty man. I don't want him corrupting all these innocent people."[8]

SIMPLY PUT: A PERSONAL COMMITMENT
TO THE SAVIOR'S WORDS

This section of Jesus' sermon is not all that difficult to understand. He speaks in terms anyone can grasp, though admittedly all may not find His words easy to accept. He speaks about marital fidelity and verbal integrity. So let's summarize His teaching with a couple of practical suggestions.

The first has to do with marriage. *Marry for all of life or do not marry for all your life.* Whatever state you are in right now, make that a vow before God. Tell the Lord you want to do that: "For the rest of my life, Lord, I don't want to marry unless I can marry for all of my life." Keep it that simple and you may be surprised how that statement will uncomplicate your love life.

The second suggestion has to do with your words: *Say what you mean and mean what you say.* It is just that simple. No mumbo jumbo, no long, drawn-out, religious-sounding stuff is necessary. Just talk truth.

CHAPTER SIX

Simple Advice to the Selfish
and Strong-Willed

LAST WEEK I heard about a traveler who, between flights at an airport, bought a small package of cookies. She then sat down in the busy snack shop to glance over the newspaper. As she read her paper, she became aware of a rustling noise. Peeking above the newsprint she was shocked to see a well-dressed gentleman sitting across from her, helping himself to her cookies. Half-angry and half-embarrassed, she reached over and gently slid the package closer to her as she took one out and began to munch on it.

A minute or so passed before she heard more rustling. The man had gotten another cookie! By now there was only one left in the package. Though flabbergasted, she didn't want to make a scene so she said nothing. Finally, as if to add insult to injury, the man broke the remaining cookie into two pieces, pushed one piece across the table toward her with a frown, gulped down his half, and left without even saying thank you. She sat there dumbfounded.

Some time later when her flight was announced, the woman opened her handbag to get her ticket. To her shock, there in her purse was her package of unopened cookies. And somewhere in that same airport was another traveler still trying to figure out how that strange woman could have been so forward and insensitive. Assumptions are shaky things to rely on; situations are not always as they appear.

It would be easy to assume that a nation as advanced and civilized as ours would be full of nothing but kind and courteous people. Furthermore, with roots that go back to God-fearing forefathers and freedom-loving ancestors, certainly those attitudes must prevail. How easy to assume that we are all a people of righteous zeal, respect for authority, uncompromising integrity, and a humble, submissive spirit. After all, anyone who reads the moving biographies of the great men and women who shaped our country and gave us our proud heritage could easily think that we still model those godly ways. As much as we may wish that to be true, it is an inaccurate assumption.

The wholesale breakdown in integrity and the national collapse of a high moral standard are now shamefully notorious in our land. In place of gentle grace and an unselfish willingness to share, it is not uncommon to encounter snarling defiance and strong-willed independence. Of course, there are exceptions, but therein lies the tragedy—they are the *exceptions*. Whoever assumes otherwise has taken up mental residence in Fantasyland.

OUR DOG-EAT-DOG MENTALITY

Without wishing to come off as a doomsayer, I am convinced we are on a downward spiral. The slogans we have become accustomed to hearing are somewhere between disappointing and disgusting. To name only a few:

- "I've got my rights."
- "I'm looking out for number one."
- "Do unto others before they do unto you."
- "Shoot first . . . ask questions later."
- "It's none of your business."
- "I don't get mad, I get even."

I can still remember when the family I grew up in moved from the sleepy little South Texas town of El Campo to the sprawling industrial city of Houston. The Second World War had begun only a few weeks before we moved. My dad, a few years too old to qualify for the military draft, felt it was his duty to leave a successful career in the insurance business and work in one of the many "defense plants," industries that set aside their civilian products and retooled their shops to contribute to the national war machine. His patriotism eclipsed what little bit of greed he may have possessed, as all five of us left the safe, secure, and simple lifestyle of a small town and slipped quietly into the harsh and often ugly realities of the big city, which back then held the dubious distinction of being the murder capital of the nation. It was frightening, to say the least.

My folks had a few friends in Houston with whom they spent some of their leisure hours, rare though they were. On one occasion their conversation turned to the strong contrast between the easygoing, gentle life in tiny El Campo and the fast-lane, sometimes-brutal environment of huge Houston—especially East Side Houston, where we lived for many years. My mother frequently repeated the words of one particular lady who warned that we would never find in the big city what we had left in our little protected hometown, adding, "It's more of a dog-eat-dog mentality here . . . and heaven help you if you forget that it can eat you up. Be careful!" She couldn't have been more correct in her evaluation. What I find disturbing, some fifty years later, is that those things which once characterized only the larger cities of America are now woven through the fabric of our society. The laid-back style of yesteryear has eroded into the fight-back world of today. A few quiet pockets of peace and innocent contentment may still exist, but no one can deny they are few and far between. Horrible acts of violence are commonplace, and the crime rate is on the rise. A recent

USA Today headline read, "7 cities lead violence 'epidemic.' " The article stated:

> Violent crime in the USA soared 10 percent in 1990—with seven cities accounting for more than a quarter of the slayings reported to FBI.
>
> The dramatic surge in violent crimes, 21 percent since 1987, continues to be driven by drug trafficking, experts say.
>
> "The nation has got to wake up to the fact that we're in an epidemic of violence," says Barry Krisberg, National Council on Crime and Delinquency.[1]

Ours is a selfish and strong-willed society. Law-enforcement agencies record it, the news media reports it, but our real need is to solve it . . . but how? Idealistic though my response may seem, I firmly believe the best answers are found in Jesus' words, which He spoke more than nineteen centuries ago. His simple advice to selfish and strong-willed humanity remains powerful and effective to this day. Be ready for a surprise, however. Most folks would never even consider following His instructions.

CHRIST'S COUNTERCULTURAL COUNSEL

In my opinion, Jesus' words recorded in Matthew 5:38–48, are among the most unusual He ever uttered. The strange-sounding advice not only cuts cross-grain against our human nature, it also represents the antithesis of the advice most Americans are given. Nevertheless, His words are wise and His way is right. If we will only give them a chance, we will discover how true and—yes, once again—how *simple* His advice really is.

He begins by quoting one of the oldest laws in the history of civilization: "You have heard that it was said, 'AN EYE FOR AN EYE, AND A TOOTH FOR A TOOTH' " (Matt. 5:38). At first glance it seems that Jesus is drawing that statement from the Mosaic Law. He certainly had the writings of Moses in mind, but that was not the first time such words had been heard by humanity. Jesus was citing the oldest law in the world—an eye for an eye and a tooth for a tooth. The original concept first occurred in the Code of Hammurabi, who ruled over Babylon from 2285 to 2242 B.C. To quote part of it:

> If a man has caused the loss of a gentleman's eye, his eye one shall cause to be lost. If he has shattered a gentleman's limb, one shall shatter his limb. . . . If he has made the tooth of a man . . . fall out, one shall make his tooth fall out.[2]

Progressing in time to the days of the Mosaic Law, we read similar words:

> But if there is any further injury, then you shall appoint as a penalty life for life, eye for eye, tooth for tooth, hand for hand, foot for foot, burn for burn, wound for wound, bruise for bruise.   Exodus 21:23–25

And if a man injures his neighbor, just as he has done, so it shall be done to him: fracture for fracture, eye for eye, tooth for tooth; just as he has injured a man, so it shall be inflicted on him.   Leviticus 24:19-20

Thus you shall not show pity; life for life, eye for eye, tooth for tooth, hand for hand, foot for foot.   Deuteronomy 19:21

So when Jesus begins, "You have heard," indeed they had. What they had been taught was retribution of the first order. Don't misunderstand. God has never upheld senseless or unjust violence, certainly not mindless brutality. However, He did establish capital punishment as the means of dealing swiftly, firmly, and thoroughly with those who acted out their violence on the innocent. As I understand Scripture, it is still the correct method of dealing with murderers. But Jesus goes further as He addresses several of the "rights" that we, in our human nature, cling to. First, familiarize yourself with what Jesus actually said:

But I say to you, do not resist him who is evil; but whoever slaps you on your right cheek, turn to him the other also. And if anyone wants to sue you, and take your shirt, let him have your coat also. And whoever shall force you to go one mile, go with him two. Give to him who asks of you, and do not turn away from him who wants to borrow from you.   Matthew 5:39-42

Do you detect certain "rights" in His words? Let me suggest four:

- My "right" to dignity . . . to be treated without insult
- My "right" to comfort . . . to cling to what pleases me
- My "right" to privacy . . . to do only what I prefer
- My "right" to possessions . . . to keep all I wish

Release Instead of Resist

Look over the list. Pretty impressive, pretty important, I'm sure you would agree.

Let any of those so-called rights be threatened today, and I can assure you somebody will soon be talking to a lawyer. Interestingly, Jesus doesn't offer that as His game plan. To the shock of His hearers then and now, He urges all of His followers to release instead of resist.

Now let me clarify something before I go any further. Please do not misapply these principles and assume they are appropriate in a national context. They aren't. At no place in our Lord's message does He address the government of a nation. This is not counsel for our national defense. This is personal admonition for the Christian, not military strategy for combat-ready forces in the field. Government's job is not the same as the Christian's job. The Christian is to follow the teachings of Jesus Christ *as an individual.* Government has a basic law of protecting its constituency, its people, and thereby serving it well. Jesus is speaking to individuals on the mountain, not to the nation in general. If they claim to follow Him, He is telling them how to do that. This is to all Christians who claim to be followers of the Way, who wish to embrace Christ's will in their lives. In Jesus' words I find four specific things His followers are to release:

First: *Release your right to personal dignity.* Now look again at how He said it. "Do not resist him who is evil; but whoever slaps you on your right cheek, turn to him the other also" (Matt. 5:39).

Even back in Jesus' day there were words that meant punching someone in the mouth and knocking him into the middle of next week. Jesus does not use those words here. He chooses other terms deliberately and for a reason. A slap on the cheek was a first-century way of insulting someone. A slap on the other cheek was yet another insulting comment, especially true in the East, where the back of the hand was a statement of insult. It wasn't the same as a doubled-up fist thrown directly into the mouth of another person. Notice that Jesus deliberately refers to a slap on the cheek.

"That was a backhanded compliment if I've ever heard one," we say today. That's our way of saying someone has made an insulting remark.

Just as we did not take plucking out the eye and cutting off the hand in a literal sense, neither do we take the slap of a hand as a literal blow to the cheek. What

Jesus is getting at is an insulting expression. If we are good at anything in our fight-back, get-even society, we are good at slapping others with insults.

None was better at insults than Winston Churchill, who had no love affair with Lady Astor. Actually, the feeling was mutual. It's reported that on one occasion she found the great statesman rather obviously inebriated in a hotel elevator. With cutting disgust she snipped, "Sir Winston, you are drunk!" to which he replied, "M'lady, you are *ugly*. And tomorrow I will be sober." That may be a classic example of how *not* to handle an insult.

Unfortunately, the more you do it, the better you get at it. And some of us are very good at it! We can make one person's sarcastic jab look mild compared to our back-of-the-hand insulting retort. Christ's simple advice? "Don't. Rather, turn the other cheek."

Insulting retaliations are not always verbal. Some of the worst occur in our driving when we are on the freeway and some self-appointed A. J. Foyt races in front of us, cuts us off, and misses hitting us by one coat of paint. The roadhog is reckless, careless, and thoughtless. What do we do? Our first thought is never, *Bless you, my son.* We usually wait for a tiny open space in the next lane so we can squirt up next to him . . . and what? *Cut him off!* (Or hope that some burly trucker in an eighteen-wheeler will cut him off before we get there.) That is just the way it is in human nature.

I think it is worth noting that our Lord suggested

two cheeks . . . not dozens of them, lest we become a doormat to the abusive. I am not the first to notice that. A successful Irish boxer was converted and became a preacher. He happened to be in a new town setting up his evangelistic tent when a couple of tough thugs noticed what he was doing. Knowing nothing of his background, they made a few insulting remarks. The Irishman merely turned and looked at them. Pressing his luck, one of the bullies took a swing and struck a glancing blow on one side of the ex-boxer's face. He shook it off and said nothing as he stuck out his jaw. The fellow took another glancing blow on the other side. At that point the preacher swiftly took off his coat, rolled up his sleeves, and announced, "The Lord gave me no further instructions." *Whop!*

Charles Haddon Spurgeon said, "We are to be the anvil when bad men are the hammers." We are to take the blows of bad men's words. Let them glance off you. But be assured, nowhere in Scripture are we instructed to be submissive doormats to rapists, silent victims of sexual or physical abuse, or helpless pawns in the hands of a would-be murderer.

> Christ's illustrations are not to be taken as the charter for any unscrupulous tyrant, beggar, or thug. His purpose was to forbid revenge, not to encourage injustice, dishonesty, or vice. . . . True love . . . takes action to deter evil and to promote good. . . . He teaches not the irresponsibility which encourages evil but the forbearance which renounces revenge.[3]

Some have taken this verse to ridiculous extremes and promoted an indifferent pacifism. If they had their way, brutal bullies would dominate our lives and dictatorial tyrants would rule the land. Martin Luther described one such pacifist as "the crazy saint who let lice nibble at him and refused to kill any of them on account of this text, maintaining that he had to suffer and could not resist evil."

If you have roaches (or lice!), don't twist Jesus' words into a persuasive plea for letting them live on, untouched. Likewise, if you have rats, poison those suckers! Furthermore, if our nation encounters an enemy who would steal our liberty, there is nothing in this that even implies we should let that enemy conquer us.

But the slap on the face is clearly an insulting comment. Release your right to answer back. When you do, you not only simplify the conflict, you usually discover that the verbal conflict ends as quickly as it began.

Second: *Release your right to cling to comforts.* Jesus said, "If anyone wants to sue you, and take your shirt, let him have your coat also" (Matt. 5:40).

This is not modern-day courtroom counsel, remember; this is personal counsel to the Christian. In this case, the man was rather well off, since he had both shirt and coat. Many lived with only a shirt. The coat was actually a cloak that was worn around the body much like a blanket; at night it was used something like a temporary sleeping bag. The human tendency was to cling to one's coat. But Jesus says here, "Let him have your coat also."

We live in an era when we have our rights to have any comfort we wish and let the rest of the world eat cake! Jesus is saying, "Those are not My words. My followers are to be moved over the needs of others and to release whatever is needed without selfishness."

When you give someone your coat, most folks won't understand you. Christ says, "Why not share? Release your rights to cling to comforts. Nothing wrong with having comforts, just don't cling to them." As I've said for years, there is absolutely nothing wrong with owning nice things, but something is terribly wrong when those nice things own us.

Third: *Release your rights to your own private lifestyle.* In Jesus' day it was not uncommon for citizens to feel the flat side of a Roman spear on their shoulder and hear some gruff-voiced soldier behind them commanding, "Pick up this package and carry it. Carry it for the next mile."

Jesus says, "Whoever shall force you to go one mile, go the second." I would imagine that back then there was some kind of saying like, "Take it a mile if they require a mile—5,280 feet—*but don't go one more foot.*" But Jesus says, "Go the extra mile." (That's where we get the expression.) By the way, the same term, translated "force" is rendered "compel" later on when Simon of Cyrene is "compelled" to carry the cross of Jesus. Isn't that interesting? Aren't you glad he picked it up? Looking back in a few days, I'm sure *he* was! Jesus says, "Don't just go the required distance. Double it."

We need to remember that Christ does not limit this to church life and Christian circles. It also applies beautifully where you are employed, especially if you are in a people-related business. There is something more important than quitting time. There is something more important than your getting every little second of your lunch hour. There is something wonderfully Christian about someone who goes beyond what is expected just as a habit of life. I want to assure you that if you live a lifestyle like this, you won't need to send out a search warrant for an audience of unbelievers who are interested in the gospel. They will seek you out!

Christ never ordered an evangelistic campaign; the crowd came to Him, not so much because He did miracles, but because He was Himself miraculous. He lived a miraculously different life. He not only modeled unselfishness, He carried a cross. He took the blows and never answered back. And aren't you glad He did? You want to simplify your faith? Release your right to a lifetime of uninterrupted privacy.

Fourth: *Release your right to exclusive ownership.* Jesus said, "Give to him who asks of you, and do not turn away from him who wants to borrow from you" (Matt. 5:42). Do you have something someone else can use? Why not share it? I never knew how many friends

I had till I owned a pickup truck. The books I have lost in letting people borrow them could probably make up a small library. And I'm sure a few of the books in my library have somebody else's name on them.

Sure, occasionally you may get ripped off. No doubt a few people will take advantage of you. I have never met a generous person yet who wasn't occasionally taken advantage of. But I've never met a truly generous person who kept score . . . or decided, "since a few don't play fair, I'm knocking this off." Every generous person I know is a person of relentless optimism. Don't let the few ripoffs make you bitter.

But is Jesus suggesting indiscriminate giving? I don't think so. William Barclay's answer to that question is probably the best I've ever read:

> The Rabbis loved to point out that loving-kindness was one of the very few things to which the Law appointed no limit at all.
>
> Are we then to say that Jesus urged upon men what can only be called indiscriminate giving? The answer cannot be given without qualification. It is clear that the effect of the giving on the receiver must be taken into account. Giving must never be such as to encourage him in laziness and in shiftlessness, for such giving can only hurt. But at the same time it must be remembered that many people who say that they will only give through official channels, and who refuse to help personal cases, are frequently merely producing an excuse for not giving at all, and are removing the personal element from giving altogether.[4]

So then—to simplify the issue at hand, Jesus says to release instead of resist. As we do, He somehow takes up the slack.

There is one more piece of advice in this section of Jesus' message. It is:

Love Instead of Hate

Love has been called the most effective motivational force in all the world. When love is at work in us, it is remarkable how giving and forgiving, understanding and tolerant we can be. It is easy to assume that power is always at work within us, but it's not. It is there, ready to be put to use, but it gets blocked. Since this has always been true, the first-century scribes and Pharisees developed a "saying," sort of a slogan that was commonly repeated among the Jews. It sounded like one of Moses' commandments, but it was a distortion instead. Jesus quoted it here: "You have heard that it was said, 'YOU SHALL LOVE YOUR NEIGHBOR, and hate your enemy'" (Matt. 5:43). The first half of that saying did appear in the Law (Lev. 19:18), but the latter half was a pharisaical addendum. Now, those Pharisees knew better. They knew that Proverbs 25:21 was in the Book:

> If your enemy is hungry, give him food to eat;
> And if he is thirsty, give him water to drink.

That and other similar statements appear in the Old Testament. But none of those statements concluded "and hate your enemy." So in order to correct the fallacy of such strong-willed reasoning, Jesus taught:

> But I say to you, love your enemies, and pray for those who persecute you in order that you may be sons of your Father who is in heaven; for He causes His sun to rise on the evil and the good, and sends rain on the righteous and the unrighteous. For if you love those who love you, what reward have you? Do not even the tax-gatherers do the same? And if you greet your brothers only, what do you do more than others? Do not even the Gentiles do the same?   Matthew 5:44-47

It may help to simplify Jesus' revolutionary counsel by observing what He does *not* say. "Love the way your enemies live." No, He does not say that. How about, "Love their methods . . . defend their ways?" Again, no. None of that appears in His statement. We are talking about people, eternal souls, spiritually blind men and women who know nothing of Christ's power.

True love possesses the ability to see beyond. In that sense we might say that love has X-ray vision. It goes beyond mere words. It sees beneath the veneer. Love focuses on the soul. Love sees another's soul in great need of help and sets compassion to work. I think of the late Corrie ten Boom and her response to the Nazi guards who had brutalized her sister. She was able to forgive them. She refused to live the rest of her life brimming with resentment and bitterness. True love sees beyond the treatment that it endures. True love doesn't need agreement to proceed. True love goes on against all odds. That is why Jesus simply says, "Love them."

I am intrigued by the sentence construction in verse 45: "in order that you may be sons of your Father." Why doesn't He say, "in order that you may be Christians"? or "in order that you may be My followers"?

I imagine Matthew, who recorded this, was among the group who first heard Jesus' sermon. Naturally he would remember the words Jesus used, even the phrases. Since Jesus spoke Aramaic, His words were more akin to Hebrew than the Greek that became the basis of the New Testament. Hebrew is not a language rich in adjectives. Instead of saying, "He is a peaceful man," the Hebrews would usually say, "He is a son of peace." Instead of saying, "She is a kind woman," the Hebrews would often say, "She is a daughter of kindness." Here, notice that Jesus says, "in order that you may be sons of your Father." May I rephrase it? "In order that you may be Fatherlike." Very seldom do we use the word "Fatherlike," but it fits here. Those who love like God begin to model a Fatherlike response . . . even toward the unrighteous. And the most Fatherlike response of all? Love.

A driving rainstorm in an area suffering from drought does not discriminate. All receive the benefits.

The same can be said for the sun. It bathes all homes alike with warmth and light. Why? Because God is love. Grace is His style. That is why Christ would minister so graciously to those who hated Him. Love and grace prompt the rain to fall on all the ground and the sun to shine on all the homes. For love to replace hate and grace to replace prejudice, playing favorites must cease. Love and grace befit those who are Fatherlike.

Next, consider the words Jesus spoke: "And if you greet your brothers only, what do you do more than others? Do not even the Gentiles do the same?" (Matt. 5:47). The Gentiles were considered the "dogs" of the human race; yet even they loved those who loved them. Likewise the tax collectors. (I won't even tell you what they called the tax collectors. There just wasn't a synonym for them that you could say in public.) Then how far do we take this love-your-neighbor stuff? Do we love atheists? Yes! Scoffers? Yes! Criminals? Yes! There would never have been a Prison Fellowship if a man named Chuck Colson had not seen beyond the bars and the hateful things men and women do. Love, remember, sees the soul and focuses on the heart.

As far back as 1880, A. F. C. Vilmar wrote:

> This commandment, that we should love our enemies and forgo [*sic*] revenge will grow even more urgent in the holy struggle which lies before us and in which we partly have already been engaged for years. In it love and hate engage in mortal combat. It is the urgent duty of every

Christian soul to prepare itself for it. The time is coming when the confession of the living God will incur not only the hatred and the fury of the world, for on the whole it has come to that already, but complete ostracism from "human society," as they call it. The Christians will be hounded from place to place, subjected to physical assault, maltreatment and death of every kind. We are approaching an age of widespread persecution. Therein lies the true significance of all the movements and conflicts of our age. Our adversaries seek to root out the Christian Church and the Christian faith because they cannot live side by side with us, because they see in every word we utter and every deed we do, even when they are not specifically directed against them, a condemnation of their own words and deeds. They are not far wrong. They suspect too that we are indifferent to their condemnation. Indeed they must admit that it is utterly futile to condemn us. We do not reciprocate their hatred and contention, although they would like it better if we did, and so sink to their own level. And how is the battle to be fought? Soon the time will come when we shall pray, not as isolated individuals, but as a corporate body, a congregation, a Church: we shall pray in multitudes (albeit in relatively small multitudes) and among the thousands and thousands of apostates we shall loudly praise and confess the Lord who was crucified and is risen and shall come again. And what prayer, what confession, what hymn of praise will it be? It will be the prayer of earnest love for these very sons of perdition who stand around and gaze at us with eyes aflame with hatred, and who have perhaps already raised their hands to kill us. It will be prayer for the peace of these erring, devastated and bewildered souls, a prayer for the same love and peace which we ourselves enjoy, a prayer which will penetrate to the depths of their souls and rend their hearts more grievously than anything they can do to us. Yes, the Church which is really waiting for its Lord, and which discerns the signs of the times of decision, must fling itself with its utmost power and with the panoply of its holy life into this prayer of love.[5]

What maturity for one to give that kind of counsel!

Can you begin to see how far we have drifted from Jesus' counsel? Don't you see why unsaved people are not really drawn to Christians? There is so little difference externally—sometimes, none at all.

Be "Perfect," Not Merely Human

As if all His other advice has not been tough enough, Jesus closes with this: "Therefore you are to be perfect, as your heavenly Father is perfect" (Matt. 5:48). Your first reaction might be one of exasperation: "Oh, give me a break!" But wait. The Lord never asks us to do the unattainable. So there must be something here we are missing. He certainly cannot mean "sinlessly perfect," an altogether impossible goal. Then what? Perhaps, "Don't be merely human; be perfect." In other words, don't operate from a faulty human philosophy, but from a divinely prescribed philosophy.

To return evil for good is devilish; to return good for good is human; to return good for evil is divine. To love as God loves is moral perfection, and this perfection Christ tells us to aim at.[6]

Jesus is urging: "Aim high–aim at perfection." But what is perfection? Perfect is from the word *telos* or *teleios*, which means not an abstract, philosophical kind of perfection, but rather *functional* perfection. In other words, to be perfect is to reach the full purpose of something or to complete the process.

If I am working on the engine on my boat and I need a certain wrench that will fit an unusual kind of nut, I may need to go to the hardware store and buy it. When I reach into the engine and the wrench fits into place, that wrench has become "perfect" in that it has fulfilled the purpose for which it was made. That is precisely what Christ's command means. Just as our heavenly Father fulfills His purpose, so should we.

SIMPLY PUT: DOING WHAT'S RIGHT

Most of us have three major realms of relationships in which we live: an immediate realm of family, an intermediate realm of friends, and a broad general realm that certainly would include some enemies.

Thinking in terms of three concentric circles, let's go first to the center and think about the family. For this I have three words of advice: *Release your rights*.

There are precious few family conflicts that cannot be settled by simply releasing rights.

I have never, never met a marriage conflict that is irreparable if both sides were equally willing to release all rights and both unhesitatingly say, "I will release my rights as I trust my God to pull us back together." If you are the selfish or strong-willed type, this will call for a radical change in attitude. I challenge you to make that change.

Second, within the intermediate circle of your friends, *look beyond the wrongs.* Every friend I have has disappointed me in one way or another. And I have done the same to him or her. But because there has been a willingness to overlook that, we still have a friendship. Love helps us stay at the task.

And finally, within the broad realm of relationships, even with your enemies, *fulfill your role.* Aim high. Be the vital wrench in their engine. Live in such a way that what you have to offer becomes a perfect fit for the things that they are missing in their lives. It is remarkable how the Lord will bring you together.

Now, for the sake of a few idealistic souls who could assume only the best and think, *I can hardly wait to live like this; this is going to be fun!* I want to bring you back ever so gently to reality. When you decide to live like Christ among the selfish and strong-willed, God will honor your decision, *but* . . . you will encounter misunderstanding and mistreatment. You will be taken advantage of. However, don't make another wrong assumption by thinking that if you are going through tough times, you are off target. Not so. Doing what is right is never a stroll through a rose garden. Jesus' plan for living may be simple, but it is not easy.

To mention only one particular area, think of confronting prejudice . . . standing for those who are objects of mistreatment. By doing so, we will please God, but we will also encounter those who hate us.

William Wilberforce stood virtually alone in England as he attempted to block slave-trading and set the blacks free. He demonstrated true Christianity, but do you know what his enemies did in return? They slandered him. They spread every kind of false rumor about him—all lies. They said he was a brutal husband. He was not. A wife beater. Never. Some passed the word that he was married secretly to a black woman. Another falsehood. He did right, but he suffered for it.

Abraham Lincoln also took up the torch against slavery during his years as our sixteenth president. The result? He became the object of hatred—and not just in the South. Some of the stories of the treatment he received from fellow Americans are beyond our comprehension. Prejudice ultimately killed him in the form of an assassin's bullet.

When Martin Luther King, Jr. began to promote his vision of nonviolence, many who were full of prejudice subjected him to incredible injustices. After King's assassination, Dr. Benjamin Mays listed some of the persecutions the man had endured. His home had been bombed. He had lived day by day, for thirteen years, under constant threats of death. He was publicly accused of being a communist. He was falsely slandered for being insincere. He was stabbed by a member of his own race. He was jailed more than twenty times. In fact, the man wrote most of his sermons in jail cells. "Love is the only force capable of transforming an enemy into a friend," he said, and he died believing that.

I'm not saying King or Lincoln or Wilberforce or any one of us who stands for something that is right but unpopular is anywhere near perfect. I'm just saying that when we live by a cause that is so different that it rebukes people, some will hate us for it. It is naïve to assume they won't. Nevertheless, let me exhort all of us to follow the teachings of Jesus Christ. No matter how painful it may be, let us trust Him to bring good from our living His way.

The Lord Jesus Christ is the model to follow—and you remember where He wound up! But think of all those who were once His enemies, now His friends. You and I would certainly be numbered among them. The force of love is absolutely unconquerable.

CHAPTER SEVEN

Beware! Religious Performance Now Showing

SINCE WE HAVE reached the halfway point in this book, you should know by now that I like things simple, especially the important things. I like simple instructions, not the kind that require a degree from MIT. I like simple meals. You know, the kind that not only taste great but also need no interpreter to analyze what you are sinking your teeth into. I also like simple evenings, preferably with members of my family or a small group of real close friends. Forcing small talk or trying to look happy while shuffling and stumbling among a couple hundred people in a crowded room is not my idea of a fun evening. Give me a fireplace, a bowl of popcorn, a little classical (or country-western) music in the background, and quiet conversation sprinkled with some laughter and even a few tears, and I'm one contented dude.

The same applies to my idea of genuine worship:

Keep it simple. I much prefer quiet, reflective times in the Lord's presence to giant meetings led by professionals who know how to work the crowd and keep the show looking good. Give me a few grand hymns mixed with several choruses of worship and spontaneous moments of silence rather than all the religious hoopla where "guest artists" take turns and crowd-pleasing singing groups share color-coordinated microphones and try to get everybody to smile and clap along with the beat. No thanks. Something within me recoils when I sense that the program is choreographed right down to the last ten seconds and I am an observer of a performance instead of a participant in worship. Don't misunderstand: I have no problem with great entertainment or professional performances. Nobody screams louder than I do at a ball game or applauds with greater enthusiasm following an evening at the symphony, but when something as meaningful and beautiful as worship gets slick or bears the marks of a complicated stage show or starts to look contrived, I start checking out the closest exits.

MICAH THE PROPHET SPEAKS

While thinking about this recently I got reacquainted with an ancient prophet named Micah. Not being one of the greater lights among the more popular prophets, Micah isn't exactly a household word. Too bad. Though obscure, the man had his stuff together.

Eclipsed by the much more famous Isaiah, who ministered among the elite, Micah took God's message to the streets.

Micah had a deep suspicion of phony religion. He saw greed in the hearts of the leaders of the kingdom of Judah, which prompted him to warn the common folk not to be deceived by religious pretense among nobility. In true prophetic style, Micah comforted the afflicted and afflicted the comfortable. He condemned sin. He exposed performance-based piety. He championed the cause of the oppressed. He predicted the fall of the nation. And he did it all at the risk of his own life.

But Micah didn't just denounce and attack, leaving everyone aware of the things he despised but none of the things he believed. Negative, ultrazealous preaching can lead people to wonder what they should do, since they hear only warnings and tirades of condemnation. Not so with Micah. Like rays of brilliant sunlight piercing charcoal-colored clouds after a storm, the prophet saved his best words for a positive message to the people. Immediately on the heels of the Lord's indictment of His people—about the time many must have begun to wonder what they had to do to make things right—Micah told them, and I am pleased to say that he did it with simplicity.

Using the time-honored method of questions and answers, he asked not one but four questions, each with greater intensity than the previous one (Mic. 6:6–7):

With what shall I come to the Lord
And bow myself before the God on high?

    [That is precisely what many were and are still wondering.]

Shall I come to Him with burnt offerings,
With yearling calves?

        [Some surely asked that question: "Does God
        expect me to sacrifice one of my livestock?"]

Does the Lord take delight in thousands of rams,
In ten thousand rivers of oil?

        [Don't miss the crescendo of intensity—the possibility of pleasing God must be remote in the
        mind of some: "Is this what He requires?"]

Shall I present my first-born for my rebellious acts,
The fruit of my body for the sin of my soul?

        [The ultimate—the zenith of devotion! "Is it going to take sacrificing my oldest child . . . or
        is He demanding that I throw myself into the
        fire on the altar? Will *that* do it? Will *that* cause
        God to smile again?"]

Micah's words state exactly what many, to this day, wonder about pleasing God. Teachers and preachers have made it so sacrificial . . . so complicated . . . so extremely difficult. To them, God is virtually impossible to please. Therefore, religion has become a series of long, drawn-out, deeply painful acts designed to appease this peeved Deity in the sky who takes delight in watching us squirm.

Micah erases the things on the entire list, replacing

the complicated possibilities with one of the finest definitions of simple faith:

> He has told you, O man, what is good;
> And what does the LORD require of you
> But to do justice, to love kindness,
> And to walk humbly with your God?
>
> Micah 6:8

At the risk of overstepping proper bounds by putting God's preference in my own words: *God Likes It Simple.* He does *not* look for big-time, external displays. He does *not* require slick public performances. He does *not* expect gigantic acts of self-sacrificial heroism, seventy-hour work weeks of ministry, a calendar of exhausting activities, an endless number of church meetings, massive dedication that proves itself in going to the most primitive tribe hidden away in the densest jungle of the world. STOP!

Go back three spaces on your monotony board of religious performance. Go back and look at how you have complicated what God said so simply. What is required? Slow down and read the list aloud:

- To do justice
- To love kindness
- To walk humbly with your God

Period.

Stop and let that sink in. Don't read one more word until you can say those three lines with your eyes closed. I'm going to test you on them later, so learn them well.

Faith is not a long series of religious performances. It is not doing a pile of pious things either to keep God from being angry or to impress others with how dedicated you are. The sooner we believe that and start living like that, the quicker we will understand the true meaning of the Christian life as God planned it—and the more contented we will be. All God asks is *simple faith*.

JESUS, OUR LORD, INSTRUCTS

These things remind me of the message Jesus delivered on the mountain—a message so simple and to the point He must have sounded like Micah from centuries earlier. The times were different, as was the geography, but the basic message was the same: Jesus underscores doing justice, loving kindness, and, especially in the early part of Matthew 6, walking humbly.

Beware of This!

> Beware of practicing your righteousness before men to be noticed by them; otherwise you have no reward with your Father who is in heaven.   Matthew 6:1

In prophetlike fashion, the Messiah introduces this section of His sermon with a strong warning: *Beware!*

Of what? Had something gone wrong? Was there some danger on the loose? You better believe it! A humble, uncomplicated walk with God had been replaced by a prime-time performance of religion. It was righteousness on display . . . strut-your-stuff spirituality led by none other than the scribes and Pharisees who loved nothing more than to impress the public with their grandiose expressions of piety on parade.

Remember the Nazarene's earlier remark about righteousness?

> For I say to you, that unless your righteousness surpasses that of the scribes and Pharisees, you shall not enter the kingdom of heaven.   Matthew 5:20

He is back on that same subject, only now He gets painfully specific with His warning. I'm always interested in seeing how a particular passage is translated in the different versions of the Bible. Here are three:

> Beware of practicing your piety before men.   RSV

> Be careful not to make a show of your religion.   NEB

> Beware of doing your good deeds conspicuously to catch men's eyes.   PHILLIPS

Walking humbly with one's God was never meant to be a theatrical performance, or, as we called it when I as a kid, "showing off."

Those of us who live in the Greater Los Angeles area

have a vast choice of professional entertainment: theatrical performances, both live and on film; dinner the-
aters; theme parks like Disneyland, Knotts Berry
Farm, Magic Mountain, and a half-dozen similar spots
where we can spend a full day watching talented people
entertain audiences. But when it comes to maximum
excitement and a crowd-pleasing evening, I don't know
of any place better than the famous Forum on a night
when the Los Angeles Lakers are in town. The man
who has announced their games for almost three decades is still at it: Chick Hearn. Every few years Chick's
co-host changes—usually it's a former basketball
player—but nobody ever upstages the man at the main
mike. In a rapid-fire, staccato manner, Chick Hearn
spits out his full-court commentary faster than any
sportscaster I have ever heard. If you are stuck in your
car and can't watch the game on television, no problem. Hearn's descriptions give the listener all that is
needed to picture the game to a T. Every once in
awhile, after a perfectly executed fast break that included several bullet passes and a basket-pounding
slam dunk by one of the Lakers, Chick Hearn's voice
drowns out the Forum roar as he shouts his familiar
response, "*It's Showtime!*"

That's to be expected in the high-octane, upbeat
world of professional basketball where fans gather for
another loud and entertaining performance. The show
is supposed to be spectacular; after all, there's Magic
in the air!

But when it comes to the walk of faith, when the subject is righteousness and the object is to glorify God, beware of show-time. Or, as Micah put it, "walk humbly with your God." Jesus is not telling His followers to stop shining light. On the contrary, He said earlier, "Let your light shine." But that had to do with the kind of much-needed light that gives others hope and attracts them to the Savior so that "they glorify your Father who is in heaven." Here He is warning against displaying our devotion before others "to be noticed by them." Simple faith and showtime don't mix.

Once He sounds the warning, Jesus applies it to the three cardinal works of piety frequently paraded by the scribes and Pharisees: giving (Matt. 6:2–4), praying (6:5–15), and fasting (6:16–18). Let's consider the first two subjects in the balance of this chapter and save the third for chapter 8.

When You Give

> When therefore you give alms, do not sound a trumpet before you, as the hypocrites do in the synagogues and in the streets, that they may be honored by men. Truly I say to you, they have their reward in full. But when you give alms, do not let your left hand know what your right hand is doing that your alms may be in secret; and your Father who sees in secret will repay you.   Matthew 6:2–4

"Giving alms" in the first century was considered synonymous with "righteousness." The ancient terms for both found their origin in the same root word, and those who were considered truly righteous were people who contributed to others' needs. But, said Jesus, there's a way *not* to give alms (v. 2), and there's a right way to do it (vv. 3–4).

It may help to know that the Pharisees had a little ritual they went through when they gave money to the poor. Whether in the synagogues or the streets, as they proceeded toward the offering container they were preceded by trumpeters who literally blew a loud fanfare. If Chick Hearn had been living back then, it would have been appropriate for him to shout, "It's Showtime, folks!"

Perhaps the Pharisees excused their self-righteous action by saying it was to attract the attention of the poor and give them new hope. We're back to that old Greek word for such rationalization: *Hogwash!* On another occasion one of their contemporaries came right out and exposed their hidden motive, saying, "they loved the approval of men rather than the approval of God" (John 12:43).

And Charles Spurgeon's comment is classic: "To stand with a penny in one hand and a trumpet in the other is the posture of hypocrisy."

That last word, "hypocrisy," though often used, is not fully appreciated without an understanding of its etymology. In classical Greek, the root term *hypocrites* was first applied to an orator and then to an actor. Figuratively, the word was used to refer to anyone who treated the world as a stage on which he played a part. No longer himself, the "hypocrite" impersonated someone he was not. That was perfectly acceptable in theatrical performances where, in ancient days, the actor wore an mask. The trouble with the religious hypocrite, however, is that he or she deliberately sets out to deceive others.

So much for how not to give. What does Jesus say about how we should give? If I read His instructions correctly, I find three primary guidelines to follow.

- Give spontaneously (not letting your left hand know what your right hand is doing).
- Give secretly (that is, anonymously).
- Give with purity of motive, knowing your heavenly Father will reward you. Count on it!

Some would argue that this makes giving mercenary. I disagree. If it were, why would Jesus mention it? Furthermore, He does not tell us how we shall be rewarded, nor should we think all His rewards will be tangible. I think C. S. Lewis is on to something when he writes this about kinds of rewards:

> There are different kinds of rewards. There is the reward which has no natural connection with the things you do to earn it and is quite foreign to the desires that ought to accompany those things. Money is not the natural reward of love; that is why we call a man mercenary if he

marries a woman for the sake of her money. But marriage is the proper reward for a real lover, and he is not mercenary for desiring it. . . . The proper rewards are not simply tacked on to the activity for which they are given, but are the activity itself in consummation.[1]

So then, what could be God's "reward" to us? Certainly the inner joy, the sheer delight in knowing that one's gift helped meet a need—someone hungry was fed, someone sick was given medical assistance, someone in vocational Christian work was encouraged to stay at the task. Great "secret joys" follow generous secret gifts.

Before Easter of 1991, several anonymous individuals in our congregation contributed to the refurbishing of our large worship center, including our adjacent chapel, choir rehearsal room, and a sizable room where we conduct adult classes and hold receptions for smaller weddings. We really needed new carpet, new pew coverings, new robes, new chairs, new paint work, and new hymnals. The congregation at large had no idea this plan was under way, nor did we ever announce either the names or amounts of money each contributor gave. Once the full amount was available, the color choices were made, fabric and carpet were selected, and the furnishings were ordered. Bright and early on a prearranged Monday morning our main building was swarming with workmen who began the project. As each day of the week passed, those of us in leadership smiled with excitement, knowing that on the next Sunday a very surprised congregation would walk into an entirely refurbished place of worship.

Sunday arrived . . . and did we have a great time! Best of all, there was no trumpet fanfare, no names were splashed up front in lights, no bronze plaques or sculptured busts on pedestals were displayed for all to see. No, there was only praise to God for the beautiful new "facelift" provided by fewer than a dozen folks who chose to give in simple faith, over and above their regular offerings. As I ministered on that delightful "surprise Sunday," I couldn't help but notice a special look of quiet delight on the faces of those who had given so generously. Because they refused to "sound a trumpet . . . that they may be honored by men," their heavenly Father had already begun to repay them.

When You Pray

And when you pray, you are not to be as the hypocrites; for they love to stand and pray in the synagogues and on the street corners, in order to be seen by men. Truly I say to you, they have their reward in full. But you, when you pray, *go into your inner room, and when you have shut your door*, pray to your Father who is in secret, and your Father who sees in secret will repay you. And when you are praying, do not use meaningless repetition, as the Gentiles do, for they suppose that they will be heard for their many words. Therefore do not be like them; for your

Father knows what you need, before you ask Him.
Matthew 6:5–8 (emphasis mine)

As before, Jesus talks briefly about what *not* to do, then spends more time on what *to* do when we pray. Make no mistake here, Jesus was certainly not discouraging prayer any more than He was discouraging giving earlier. What He spoke against was playing the role of a hypocrite when going through the motions of prayer. Thanks to the professional show-offs of the day, prayer had become formal, repetitive, regulated, and overdone . . . another tragic practice of religion on display. Using their example, hypocritical to the core, we are able to discern what not to do when we pray:

- Do not be hypocritical
- Do not seek to be seen while praying
- Do not limit your praying to public places
- Do not use meaningless repetition

Putting prayer on display is one of the most obvious and obnoxious acts of hypocrisy we can engage in. If you have ever done so, determine from this moment on never again to make prayer a public performance. This intimate act of worship must never be abused. How often I hear (and occasionally participate in!) long, wordy, self-serving acts of intercession where prayer becomes the vehicle for transporting loads of theological jargon and eloquent, pious phrases uttered to impress. Let's stop it!

Then what should we do instead? Jesus tells us.

First: *Find a private place to be alone.* He is talking about private devotions here, not public prayers. Get away. "Shut your door." Deliberately do not let it be known that you are meeting alone with God. You have no quiet place? How about your car? When our busy family was growing up, my mother preferred the bathroom. That door even has a lock. Go in. Be quiet. Pour out your soul.

Second: *Pray to your heavenly Father in secret.* I love the words the psalmist wrote on prayer:

> When Thou didst say, "Seek My face," my heart
> said to Thee,
> "Thy face, O LORD, I shall seek."   Psalm 27:8

> He who dwells in the shelter of the Most High
> Will abide in the shadow of the Almighty.
> Psalm 91:1

Do you have a place of shelter where you seek only His face? Do you spend time in that secret place? Have you given prayer the priority it deserves? When you pray, remember it is the Lord's face you seek. I am learning as I continue in ministry that it is possible to be engaged in the work of ministry yet be in secret very, very seldom. There is this great tendency to think my best work is done at my desk or on my feet . . .

but it's really done on my knees. It is easy to become so caught up in people's needs (which are endless and usually urgent) and to be so preoccupied with meeting those needs that I miss "the shelter of the Most High." How easy to emphasize all the involvements of being with people, rather than being alone in a secret place with Him. And I do mean *alone* with God, as though there is not another care, another need, another person—only "the Almighty."

In the last year and a half, maybe two, I have begun to realize the value of this. As a result of time invested in the secret place we gain an invincible sense of God's direction and the reassurance of His hand on our lives, along with an increased sensitivity regarding iniquity in our own lives.

Being alone with God is not complicated, but it is tough to maintain. Nevertheless, we need secrecy, especially in this hyperactive, noisy, busy world of ours. Paul Tournier, in his work *Secrets*, writes:

> Every human being needs secrecy in order to become himself and no longer a member of his tribe . . . in order to collect his thoughts. . . . To respect the secrecy of whoever it may be, even your own child, is to respect his individuality. To intrude upon his private life, to violate his secrecy, is to violate his individuality. . . .
>
> So therefore, if keeping a secret was the first in the formation of the individual, telling it to a freely chosen confidant is going to constitute then the second step in the formation of the individual. He who cannot keep a secret

is not free. But he who can never reveal it is not free either.[2]

Consider the beauty, the wonder, the magnificence, the awe-inspiring times of praise in the secret place! There is nothing to be compared to it. As great as corporate worship may be, with a magnificent pipe organ and full orchestra and a congregation singing at full volume, it cannot compare to the secret place where our best work is done and where God's best work is accomplished in us. I am fully convinced that doing justice and loving kindness and walking humbly with our God simply cannot happen without sufficient time in the secret place.

Third: *Keep it simple.* God doesn't pay closer attention because we use more verbiage, nor does it take a continuous stream of repetitious words, like some mysterious mantra, to make Him sit up and take notice.

Jesus gave His listeners a simple prayer to use as a model; we call it the Lord's Prayer. Actually it is the disciples' prayer. We shall look at it in depth in the next chapter.

SIMPLY PUT: THE SPIRIT APPLIES . . .

This is a good place to stop and put all that we have considered in this chapter into perspective. Admittedly, we have covered a lot of ground, but at the heart of everything has been Jesus' warning: "Beware of religious performances!" Why? Because God is not glorified in such extravaganzas . . . and because we suffer the consequences. Three "performances," in particular, come to mind:

- When our devotion becomes an act we lapse into hypocrisy.
- When our giving lacks secrecy we lose our reward.
- When our prayers turn into demonstrations we lack God's power.

Remember Micah's threefold answer to those searching questions he asked? What is it God requires? Extensive burnt offerings? Yearling calves? Thousands of sheep? Ten thousand rivers of oil? Our firstborn? Our own lives thrown into the fire? No.

Then what? See if you can you remember.

- To do _____.
- To love _____.
- To walk _____.

That's it. That's all. Really, that's everything.

Back in 1958 when I was a young Marine stationed on the island of Okinawa, I became closely associated with a man I deeply admired. His name was Bob Newkirk. I didn't know what it was exactly that first drew me to Bob. More than anything, I guess, there was something refreshingly unpretentious about him. He was devoted to the things of the Lord, no question, but it was never on parade, never for the purpose of public display. And I loved that. Perhaps it was his balanced Christian life that I admired most. He was serving back then with The Navigators, an international Christian organization committed to ministering to military personnel. However, he never tried to squeeze me into some Navigator mold. I liked that especially. When we worked, we worked hard, but when we played, we had a first-class blast. I never got the idea that Bob was interested in making big impressions on me or other people. He was what he was, plain and simple—far from perfect, but authentic. Real.

I remember dropping by his home late one rainy evening to pay an unexpected visit. His wife met me at the door and informed me that he was not home. She added, "You've probably noticed lately that he has been under some stress. I think he may be down at his office. I'm not really sure. But he told me he just wanted to get alone."

I decided to try the office, a little spot down in Naha. I caught the three-wheel jitney that took me from the village where the Newkirks lived down to the capital city of the island. It was still raining lightly, so I stepped around and over the puddles as I made my way down a street, across an alley, then another alley until I came upon his unassuming, modest office. Before I arrived, however, I could hear singing in the distance—

> Come, Thou Fount of every blessing,
> Tune my heart to sing Thy grace.[3]

It was Bob's voice; I'd know it anywhere. I stood outside in the rain for a few moments, listening. The simple hymn continued. I confess, I peeked in the window and saw a candle on a table, my friend on his knees, and not another soul around. He was spending time with the Lord . . . all alone. As I stood outside, the soft-falling rain dripping off my nose and ears, my eyes filled with tears of gratitude. Bob never knew I came by that evening, but without his knowing it, I got a glimpse of authentic Christianity that night. Not piety on parade . . . not spiritual showtime, but a man "in the shelter of the Most High."

In the back streets of Naha I learned more about simple faith than I would later learn in four years of seminary.

CHAPTER EIGHT

Prayer and Fasting Minus
All the Pizzazz

THE ENEMY of our souls is the expert of extremes. It seems he will stop at nothing until we get out of the realm of balance and onto some lunatic fringe.

Take evangelism. Instead of adopting a lifestyle-evangelism approach where presenting the claims of Christ flows very naturally and appropriately, Christians seem to either clam up or get fanatical. If the truth were known, many believers never open their mouths regarding their faith. They are secret-service saints, not about to speak of the One who has transformed their lives. And then there are others who go temporarily nuts. They elbow their way in and offend more than they win. The problem is that neither category has learned the value of balance.

Bible study is another example. On the one hand there are Christians who virtually ignore the Scriptures all week long, then when Sunday comes they start the hunt to see where they left their Bible after church last week. And then there are those who become Bible *freaks*. They live for one purpose: to study the Scriptures. Between Bible classes, home Bible studies, Bible correspondence courses, and going part-time to a Bible college, they hardly have time for work or family. Few sights are more pathetic than a Christian who has gone overboard and doesn't realize it. The family is embarrassed, especially the kids. The neighbors are turned off. The folks at work hate to see that person coming toward them.

Having said all this, I would also be the first to say that the things of the Lord are not only thrilling, they are downright fascinating. And because scriptural truth is so profound, a bottomless pit of inexhaustible and magnificent riches, the treasure hunt through God's Word is like nothing else on earth. Having spent about forty years of my life searching through the doctrines, the theological subjects, the biblical characters, the history, and the practical application of truth to life, I can vouch for the fact that it can easily become addictive. And those most addicted are often those most preoccupied. Their heads are so into the queen of the sciences, some can hardly match their socks.

I suppose every person who has studied at a theological seminary has a story or two about a preoccupied professor. I certainly do. Usually this character is balding, wears thick glasses and baggy pants, carries a beat-up briefcase, hasn't the foggiest idea who won the World Series last week, and cannot quite remember where he parked the car that morning.

One of my esteemed mentors, I understand, once traveled from his home in Philadelphia to Baltimore for a weekend of ministry. Late Sunday evening he caught the flight back to Philly, but his wife wasn't there to meet him. He gave her a call to see why.

"Dear, where are you? I'm back. I thought you'd be here to meet me."

"To meet you? Where are you?"

"I'm here at the airport. Just flew in from Baltimore, remember?"

"The airport! Honey, you *drove* to Baltimore."

It takes a special kind of mate to be married to someone who lives in a world all his (or her) own. But since such a malady is so innocent, I suppose God gives special grace.

When the addiction leads to personal preoccupation, that is one thing. But when it leads to public ostentation, that is quite another. Webster defines ostentation as "excessive display," and therein lies the dark side of the extreme. That is what Jesus attacked with a vengeance in His immortal sermon. As you may recall, He spoke directly against making an excessive display of things like giving and praying.

A BRIEF REVIEW:
GIVE ANONYMOUSLY, PRAY SECRETLY

> Beware of practicing your righteousness before men to
> be noticed by them; otherwise you have no reward with
> your Father who is in heaven.   Matthew 6:1

You remember that warning, I'm sure. Jesus' passionate plea is not that we stop giving or praying in public, but that whenever we do either, we not make a show of it.

The Christian is to live in such a way that men looking at him, and seeing the quality of his life, will glorify God. He must always remember at the same time that he is not to do things in order that he may attract attention to himself. He must not desire to be seen of men, he is never to be self-conscious. But, clearly, this balance is a fine and delicate one; so often we tend to go to one extreme or the other. Christian people tend either to be guilty of great ostentation or else to become monks and hermits. As you look at the long story of the Christian Church throughout the centuries you will find this great conflict has been going on. They have either been ostentatious, or else they have been so afraid of self and self-glorification that they have segregated themselves from the world. But here we are called to avoid both extremes.[1]

Not wishing to leave us with a general warning but no specifics, Jesus addresses three very real areas of the Christian life: giving, praying, and fasting.

Specific Commands

"When you give. . . ." We examined this closely in the previous chapter, so there is no need to rehearse the scene again. Just keep in mind the importance of not calling attention to yourself. Give, and go on with your life.

"When you pray. . . ." Here again, no ostentation, please. Keep it quiet. Remember you are praying "to your Father," not to those who may be sitting near you. And lots of words or the same phrases used repeatedly will not get you anywhere with God. Repeated requests sound as monotonous to Him as they do to others—maybe even a little irritating.

I was at the grocery store down the street the other evening, and in a bit of a hurry. As usual, the lines were long and everyone, it seemed, was buying enough to feed the entire roster of the Los Angeles Rams. Right in front of me was a hassled mother with three small, active boys who appeared to be about ten or eleven months apart in age. The youngest was the busiest of them all. He was perched in the shopping-cart seat, leaning over toward the gum and candy bars with two outstretched arms and repeating the same line over and over again as Mama was trying to unload her cart. The other two were shoving and arguing with each other. She was trying to referee while junior kept up his pleading:

"Mama, I want some TicTacs . . . Mama, I want some TicTacs. Mama, I want some TicTacs . . . Mama, I want some TicTacs."

By now most folks in all the lines were looking in his direction, but the little guy never let up.

"Mama, I want some TicTacs. Mama, I want some TicTacs. Mama, I want some TicTacs. MAMA, I WANT SOME TICTACS. MAMAIWANTSOMETICTACS!!!"

Even though I was not "Mama," I was about to unload the case of TicTacs on the kid when Mama reached her breaking point. "NO . . . and stop asking!" she screamed in a voice that carried six stores away, I'm sure. He never stopped. Suddenly, to my surprise, she grabbed a box of TicTacs and shoved them into his hands. I then realized why the kid kept asking. He had learned that it worked!

When I returned to Jesus' words in Matthew 6:7, it dawned on me that the mindless-repetition approach may work with pagans and hassled parents, but it doesn't work with God! Endlessly repeated words may wear some parents down and force them to give in, but God tells us "do not be like them; for your Father knows what you need, before you ask Him" (6:8). God takes delight in meeting His children's needs, but His response is not based on how often we ask or how many times we use the same words. All He expects is that we come in simple faith.

FURTHER INSTRUCTION:
WHEN PRAYING . . . WHEN FASTING

Only on the rarest of occasions did Jesus ever spell out

some precise pattern to follow in any of the disciplines of piety. It is as though He left the nuts and bolts to each of His own, not expecting us to jump through a prescribed set of hoops. But here is one of the rare occasions.

"Pray, Then, in This Way"

What a model He has left us! A studied look at the whole prayer will be worth our effort.

> Pray, then, in this way:
> "Our Father who art in heaven,
> Hallowed be Thy name.
> Thy kingdom come.
> Thy will be done,
> On earth as it is in heaven.
> Give us this day our daily bread.
> And forgive us our debts, as we also have forgiven our debtors.
> And do not lead us into temptation, but deliver us from evil. [For Thine is the kingdom, and the power, and the glory, forever. Amen.]" Matthew 6:9-13

As I glance over the prayer we are to pattern ours after, the first observation that jumps out at me is that the focus is on the Lord: His person, His name, His rule, His will. Next, attention is drawn to our needs.

- Give us . . . our daily bread.

- Forgive us our debts.
- Deliver us from evil.

So simple, so clear, so easy to follow. I hope I don't complicate things as I dig a little deeper for the next few lines. Much of the prayer is self-explanatory.

To begin with, the Lord would have us address Him as "Our Father." We are living in a time when more and more Christians direct their prayers to Jesus. I do not remember any occasion in the Scriptures where people prayed to the Son of God, so I suggest we follow His instructions stated here. When He taught His followers to pray, it was always to the Father. So if you wish to be absolutely biblical about it, pray to the Father and call Him that. It will help you in praying to picture Him in your mind as Father more than Friend, or more than just a distant Deity. But of all the titles we could choose to use, Father says it best. He is our heavenly Father. He cares for His children. He knows how to handle His family.

There is both respect and freedom in the title. When there is a healthy relationship between Father and child, there is freedom. There is also openness. You can relax as you speak, yet you respect Him. And the longer I spend in the Father's presence, the less I want to tell Him what to do, and the more I want to linger in His presence.

Notice how He would have us envision Him: "who art in heaven." Literally it reads "in the heavens," for the Greek uses the plural term. This speaks of the transcendence, the immanence of God. He is in the air that surrounds us. He is in the galaxies, the multiple thousands of galaxies removed from us. He encompasses the heavens. He is not contained in the letters G-O-D. He is everywhere and yet as close as my own breath.

"Hallowed be Thy name." Hallowed is one of those terms we rarely use these days. It means consecrated, holy, dedicated.

Perhaps the most eloquent time "hallowed" flowed from English-speaking lips was when Abraham Lincoln used it in his Gettysburg Address. Looking out over the Pennsylvania fields that had been littered with the remains of thousands of brave young Americans only five months before, Lincoln said, "But, in a larger sense, we cannot dedicate, we cannot consecrate, we cannot hallow this ground. The brave men, living and dead, who struggled here, have consecrated it far above our power to add or detract."

In a similar sense, we cannot "hallow" God, but we can acknowledge that He is holy. "Hallowed be Thy name," then, is a statement of fact rather than a request. "I acknowledge, by uttering Your name, Father, that Your name is hallowed, holy, absolutely separate from sin."

By merely reviewing the first few lines of the Lord's Prayer, we gain a renewed respect . . . a healthy and wholesome sense of reverence for our Almighty God and Father. Rather than causing us to run from Him and hide in fear, I find that such an awesome respect makes me want to come close to Him, to wait quietly for Him to work. And so I urge you to slow your pace, to approach His "hallowed name" thoughtfully. Take time! Give Him the respect He deserves. Wait on God. In return, He will give you a clearer vision. Furthermore, He will soften your will and make you want to know and do His will.

The prayer continues with these familiar words: "Thy kingdom come. Thy will be done." It is as if Jesus is saying, "Let it come to pass. May it one day transpire in that grand kingdom You promised for this earth. May it be the kind of kingdom where You rule over all. In the meantime, may Your will be done on earth as it is always done among the adoring angels about You." I detect here the willing submission of one's life to the will of God. "Let Your will be done in me, whatever it may take, Lord." Simple words to say, but terribly significant.

After focusing on His heavenly person, His name, His rule, and His will, there is an appropriate shift to earthly needs: "Give us this day our daily bread." Look closely. "Daily bread" means the basics. It's not, "Give us this day our daily cake," "our daily pie," or even "our weekly feast." All we need in order to live is bread, basic sustenance. "Just enough clothing to keep me warm, Lord, just give that. Anything above that is grace. I'll settle for bread, and I need it on a daily basis." Daily bread is a symbol for everything necessary for the preservation of life.

"And while You're giving, there is something I need just as much for my inner self, Lord . . . forgiveness." What bread is to the physical being, forgiveness is to the soul. Sin is like a lingering debt. Interest accumulates. If that debt is not paid, we must bear the consequences. We cannot cover our own sins all alone. We need help from above, and the help He provides cleanses us and washes our sins away. So when we pray, let's not forget to place our debt of sin before the One who forgives it.

The part that troubles most people in the Lord's Prayer is the request, "Do not lead us into temptation." How could He? His name is hallowed. He is holy. If temptation means the solicitation to evil, how could He do that? James says,

> Let no one say when he is tempted, "I am being tempted by God"; for God cannot be tempted by evil, and He Himself does not tempt anyone. But each one is tempted when he is carried away and enticed by his own lust. Then when lust has conceived, it gives birth to sin; and when sin is accomplished, it brings forth death. James 1:13-15

Clearly, God cannot tempt anyone. Holiness never solicits evil.

Some have suggested this means, "Do not lead us into a test." But why wouldn't He? Testing breeds endurance, and through endurance we develop character. So the Lord does grant testing.

Most likely the phrase "do not lead us" is a permissive imperative and could best be rendered, "do not allow us to be led into temptation." Or better, "do not allow us to be overwhelmed by temptation," which explains why He then adds, "but deliver us from evil." I think that is a reference to the enemy himself—Satan—the evil one and his host of demons. In other words, "Lord rescue us."

Could there also be a veiled reference to the Trinity in these three levels of requests? It is the Lord our Father, our Sustainer, who gives daily bread. It is the Son, our Savior, who makes the forgiveness of debts possible through His blood. And it is the Spirit of God who is our Indweller and Rescuer.

Are you aware of what our adversary hates most about you and me? He hates the pleasure we enjoy in our Father's presence. He once enjoyed it himself. But through a series of prideful acts, he was cast out. And he looks back with despicable envy on all who enjoy the pleasure in the presence he once enjoyed, but is now separated from forever.

Thomas Watson, the seventeenth-century Puritan, put it very well: "Satan envies man's happiness. To see a cloud of dust so near to God, and himself, once a glorious angel, cast out of heavenly paradise, makes him curse mankind with inveterate hatred."

And then comes that dramatic conclusion, which has inspired such grand music: "For thine is the king-

dom, and the power, and the glory, forever. Amen."
What an appropriate ending for the prayer!

While thinking through the themes of this prayer, my mind has often returned to the theme of forgiveness. Is there any greater relief on earth than that?

Dr. Earl Palmer, a good friend and the senior pastor at the First Presbyterian Church of Berkeley, California, does a masterful job of illustrating this truth as he likens it to the Golden Gate Bridge:

> I have often thought of the Golden Gate Bridge in San Francisco as our city's boldest structure in that its great south pier rests directly upon the fault zone of the San Andreas Fault. That bridge is an amazing structure of both flexibility and strength. It is built to sway some twenty feet at the center of its one-mile suspension span. The secret to its durability is its flexibility that enables this sway, but that is not all. By design, every part of the bridge—its concrete roadway, its steel railings, its cross beams—is inevitably related from one welded joint to the other up through the vast cable system to two great towers and two great land anchor piers. The towers bear most of the weight, and they are deeply imbedded into the rock foundation beneath the sea. In other words, the bridge is totally preoccupied with its foundation. This is its secret! Flexibility and foundation. In the Christian life, it is the forgiveness of the gospel that grants us our flexibility; and it is the Lord of the gospel who is our foundation.[2]

"And Whenever You Fast"

Just as Jesus dealt with giving and praying, He now deals with fasting—how not to do it, then, how to do it. Consider, first, the negative.

> And whenever you fast, do not put on a gloomy face as the hypocrites do, for they neglect their appearance in order to be seen fasting by men. Truly I say to you, they have their reward in full.   Matthew 6:16

He tells us not to put on a gloomy face, not to neglect our appearance, and not to seek a superpious look. I believe He is saying that no one should ever be able to tell just by looking that we have been fasting. Great game plan . . . but not always followed.

Have you ever been around people who really wanted to look spiritual? They are gloom personified, apparently living out one of the unwritten laws in the ancient code of pharisaical ethics. Down through the centuries of Christianity many have cultivated that "seriously religious" appearance. It is especially popular among superpious missionaries who talk about the burden of the mission field, or among pastors who are weighed down with the burden of the pastorate. Burden? Whose burden? The ministry is *His* burden. Since that is true, what are we doing bearing His burden and trying to look so grim about it? We *ought* to be grim if we are attempting to carry what God is supposed to carry! But we are not made to carry out His role, so let's stop trying. Playing a false role promotes pride, which is easily detected.

I heard recently that a flight attendant once said to the then-heavyweight champion of the world, Muhammad Ali, "Please fasten your seat belt."

He replied with a sneer, "Superman don't need no seat belt."

"Superman don't need no airplane," she responded. "Buckle up, please."

Show-offs never miss a trick. In Jesus' day some religious show-offs even painted their faces a little whiter so they would look pale when they were fasting—not unlike an old marble statue of a saint might look standing in the dusty corner of a giant cathedral.

One of my best friends and a longstanding mentor has often said with a smile, "You can be a fundamentalist, but you don't have to look like one."

Some people think they will appear more spiritual if they look like an unmade bed . . . hair unkempt, no deodorant, no pressed clothes or shined shoes, and certainly no stylish fashions. After all, we are supposed to be citizens of heaven! That may be true, but until we get there, there are lots of folks who have to live with us on earth. Let's be considerate of them! Fasting or not, trying to look holy (whatever that means) won't cut it. In today's terms, Jesus says, "Knock it off!"

Fasting is good for one's health. Fasting helps bring perspective and break bad habits. Fasting is good for self-control. It encourages a protracted focus on Christ and a wholesome self-discipline. It gives time to let the silt of our lives drop to the bottom. It brings us back to basics. Fasting simplifies our faith. But that is also why we are never to promote it, brag about it, or display it. There should not be a conference on fasting, where everybody goes out and does it for four hours and then returns for a big supper that night.

There is an old rabbinical maxim that says: "A man will have to give an account on the judgment day for every good thing which he might have enjoyed, and did not."[3]

As the Apostle Paul put it, "God . . . richly supplies us with all things to enjoy" (1 Tim. 6:17). Yes, "all things."

Jesus Himself spoke against wearing a gloomy face and having an unkempt look to parade one's spirituality, which is not spirituality at all.

> But you, when you fast, anoint your head, and wash your face so that you may not be seen fasting by men, but by your Father who is in secret; and your Father who sees in secret will repay you.   Matthew 6:17–18

What wonderful, balanced counsel! How often our Savior must have fasted, but never once did He make a show of it.

SIMPLY PUT: PERSONAL OBEDIENCE

Jesus has touched on things that are so down to earth and so practical you would think the ink was still wet.

They could have been written this very morning. In a sense they were . . . that's the way God's Word is, always alive and active and sharp.

Now, how do we make it happen—come alive—in our lives? Let me leave with you a couple of suggestions.

First, *make the heavenly Father, not people, your main focus.* Remember the prayer pattern? "*Our Father* who art in heaven" . . . we're not praying to all the people who watch us. "Hallowed be Thy name" . . . not the folks around us—none of their names are hallowed. "*Thy* will be done . . . *Thy* kingdom come" . . . not the will of our fellow church members.

Have you allowed yourself to fall under the thumb of somebody's will? No wonder you don't enjoy life! You are taking your cues from those who frown back at you. What do they know about what God is doing in your life?

I'll be candid with you. The older I get the less I worry about what people think and the more I concern myself with what God thinks. When I get His green light, I confess, I move in that direction and He and I have the time of our lives. But, invariably, there are some people who don't understand. (Many don't want to understand.) That is why I encourage others to focus on Him. I strongly suggest you do the same. But watch out . . . it will change your life.

Second: *Make the secret place, not the public place, your primary platform.* You want a safe place to spend more time? Choose the secret place. Spend more time there and less time seeking the public platform. In that secret place you will find a quiet depth and a courageous invincibility that is nothing short of contagious.

CHAPTER NINE

When Simple Faith Erodes

LAST NIGHT was wonderful. It was more than that; it was memorable. It had all the ingredients of a never-to-be-duplicated evening. Long-term friends. Nostalgic reminders. Laughter and a few tears. Words of gratitude. Authentic expressions of praise to God. Glorious music. Well-chosen remarks from sincere hearts. Choice comments in print . . . the works! Cynthia and I were treated to a delightful evening at our church where the congregation gathered to say, "Thank you for twenty years of ministry among us." It was hard to believe that twenty years had already passed.

We were urged to sit back, relax, and accept everything that was planned in our honor. And though neither of us feels all that comfortable in the center of such celebrations, we were reminded more than once that we needed to have "the grace to receive" (sound familiar?) what people wanted to do for us and say to us. To God went the glory—no question about that—but to my wife and me came the most overwhelming

173

expressions of affirmation we have ever received. Because it was handled so appropriately, so lovingly, and because nothing said or done represented flattery, but rather respect and true gratitude, Cynthia and I left with misty eyes and joyful hearts.

The theme was "Thanking God for the First Twenty Years." I suppose there was a hint of job security in that phrase, so that alone was encouraging. But the best part of all was looking into the faces of many of the most significant and cherished people in our lives and realizing how interwoven our paths have been during these two decades we have journeyed together. I will never forget those faces. Each one reflected absolute honesty, genuine respect, and, yes, simple faith . . . but most of all a deep trust that has been building over the past twenty years.

I didn't sleep much through the night. Those faces kept passing in review, faces that smiled and said, "We trust you . . . We believe in you." Unless I miss my guess, those same faces were also saying, "Stay true . . . continue to give us reasons to trust you, to respect and believe in you . . . keep growing; but as the years of the future pass, don't drift, Chuck. As you have done for us in the past, give our children the memory of a minister they can trust. Stay strong. Remain pure, dear friend. Don't fake it . . . don't start covering up secret sins that will one day turn to scandal." Understand, no one actually said those words, but as I lay there awake, looking at the moonlit ceiling, that's what I heard.

It is an awesome thing to be trusted. Respect, though so very important, hangs on terribly thin wires. And what makes it all so fragile is that there is nothing in the mere passing of time that automatically strengthens the fiber of one's character. As a matter of fact, each day we live there are subtle opportunities inviting us to let up, to compromise. Nothing boisterous and bold, you understand, but little things, secret things, that wink and flirt and invite us in. It is like erosion—never obvious or quick or announced. One of my esteemed mentors of yesteryear, the late Dr. Richard H. Seume, had an eloquent description for it: "the lure of a lesser loyalty."

No guarantees accompany a minister's second twenty years in the same place. If anything, they are tougher. A maintenance mentality can emerge as zeal fades. Rationalization can accompany slight slips and within a matter of time secret sins, like undetected melanoma, begin to take their toll. The categories are legion. We usually think first of being lured into sexual compromise, a very real and common area of enemy attack, but it is only one of many possibilities. Greed is equally subtle. The same could be said of pride or unaccountability or lust for power . . . jealousy of the younger and more gifted, the tendency to become manipulative or overly dogmatic, negative or self-serving . . . or just plain slothful, relying on yesterday's study and last year's sermons. I dare not miss mentioning the hidden snare of cynicism or an attitude of presumption. The supple, teachable years of our youth can erode, leaving us brittle, boastful, or even bitter. And learning to cover all that up comes easier with the passing of time. Ever so slowly a life of refreshingly simple faith can become tainted and tortured within, before anyone knows it is happening.

THE TRAGEDY OF SETTLING FOR LESS

None of the above is new. The roots of secret erosion go deep into the soil of humanity; some of these cases are so notorious they have found their way into the biblical record. Elisha's trusted servant comes to mind. Quiet, faithful, and loyal to the prophet, Gehazi entertained private thoughts of materialistic greed. Who would ever have guessed? Nothing external sounded an alarm . . . but when the test came, the once-trusted servant was trapped.

And then there was King David's own General Joab, tenacious in battle and a time-honored friend, who started strong but ended weak. This man of military might died in dishonor and was buried, not in Israel's equivalent to Arlington National Cemetery with full military honors alongside other national heroes, but by a cabin in the wilderness. What happened to Joab?

How could he have done such a thing? Chalk up another one for erosion.

And Demas—we dare not omit his sad scriptural obituary from Paul's pen: "Demas, having loved this present world, has deserted me." A trusted friend, no doubt a traveling companion who once talked and prayed with Paul, who knew the hardship and heartaches of ministry as well as delightful moments of accomplishment shared together, was lured by a lesser loyalty. Tragic, indeed.

The path of the faithful is littered with the mute remains of those who once sang great songs of loudest praise before their simple faith slid into cynicism and spiritual defeat.

Oswald Chambers serves notice to all of us who tread the path of faith:

> Always remain alert to the fact where one man has gone back is exactly where anyone may go back. . . . You have gone through the big crisis, now be alert over the least things; take into calculation the "retired sphere of the leasts." [1]

I understand that one year when Dr. Will Houghton was still the president of Moody Bible Institute, he was addressing a packed auditorium during the school's Founder's Week. In the course of his message, he told of an experience he'd had some years earlier with his predecessor, Dr. James M. Gray. The two of them had been together in conference ministry, and as they parted company, they paused for a few moments of prayer. Dr. Houghton still remembered the vulnerable, unguarded petition that fell from Gray's lips that day. To his amazement, he heard his quiet and dignified colleague utter the simple prayer, "O God, don't let me become a wicked old man." There remains a warning in that to all of us: "Let him who thinks he stands take heed lest he fall" (1 Cor. 10:12). It is those "retired spheres of the leasts" that we cannot, we *dare not* ignore.

I have thought about all this a lot, not only in the last eighteen hours but for the last several years. The crucial question, I think, is this: *Why would anyone let this happen?* Nobody in his or her right mind gets up in the morning, sits on the side of the bed, and thinks, *Let's see, how can I ruin my life today? How can I break the trust of all who respect me and believe in me?* Of course not. What happens is far more subtle. Perhaps it originates with these alien thoughts: *Who will ever know? I'm absolutely safe. Furthermore, this is as far as I'll go. . . . period. Not even God concerns Himself with such small things. He's much too involved with bigger issues than this; He hardly cares . . .* Wrong! Read and reason through the following:

> The Lord looks from heaven;
> He sees all the sons of men;
> From His dwelling place He looks out
> On all the inhabitants of the earth,

He who fashions the hearts of them all,
He who understands all their works.
Psalm 33:13-15

O LORD, Thou hast searched me and known me.
Thou dost know when I sit down and when I rise up;
Thou dost understand my thought from afar.
Thou dost scrutinize my path and my lying down,
And art intimately acquainted with all my ways.
Psalm 139:1-3

For the eyes of the LORD move to and fro throughout the earth that He may strongly support those whose heart is completely His. You have acted foolishly in this. Indeed, from now on you will surely have wars.
2 Chronicles 16:9

And there is no creature hidden from His sight, but all things are open and laid bare to the eyes of Him with whom we have to do.   Hebrews 4:13

While I am mentioning all this scriptural evidence, do you remember what we heard from Jesus' lips in the previous chapter? Several times He spoke of "your Father who sees in secret" (Matt. 6:4, 6, 18). A firm belief in the omniscience of God—His knowing all things at all times—will go a long way in restraining our tendency to rationalize or think we can operate in secret. God sees it all because He cares about every single detail of our existence. The life of simple faith is a life that is lived openly before God and in willing accountability before others. If you want to complicate your life, start thinking that you can divide your world into public and private realms. That is as erroneous as telling ourselves that life can be divided into the secular and the sacred. For the one who claims to be a follower of Jesus, nothing falls under the "secular" category. When we start believing that heresy, "the lure of a lesser loyalty" only intensifies.

THE IMPOSSIBILITY OF SERVING TWO MASTERS

Returning to Jesus' profound words, we come to one of the most penetrating paragraphs of truth in the New Testament. Read His words carefully.

Do not lay up for yourselves treasures upon earth, where moth and rust destroy, and where thieves break in and steal. But lay up for yourselves treasures in heaven, where neither moth nor rust destroys, and where thieves do not break in or steal; for where your treasure is, there will your heart be also. The lamp of the body is the eye; if therefore your eye is clear, your whole body will be full of light. But if your eye is bad, your whole body will be full of darkness. If therefore the light that is in you is darkness, how great is the darkness! No one can serve two masters; for either he will hate the one and love the other, or he will hold to one and despise the other. You cannot serve God and mammon.   Matthew 6:19-24

Talk about clear communication. As I have said several times, no one was ever better at it than Jesus.

Looking over His words, it is the contrasts that stand out. I see at least four:

- Treasures upon earth . . . treasures in heaven (vv. 19–20)

- Outer/visible treasure . . . inner/invisible treasure (v. 21)

- If the eye is clear . . . if the eye is bad (vv. 22–23)

- A body full of light . . . a body full of darkness (vv. 22–23)

We'll come back to those contrasts momentarily, but first, observe how Jesus begins His remarks in contrast to the way He ends them. At the beginning He gives a strong command: "Do not . . ." (v. 19), but at the end He states a simple fact: "You cannot . . ." (v. 24). Contrasts make things crystal clear, and since He spoke these words in a culture where the master-slave relationship was commonplace, we can be certain His audience got the point, especially when He declared, "No one can serve two masters." Dual lordship is an impossibility; when we attempt to do the impossible, the life of simple faith degenerates into maximum complications.

To put it in the simplest of terms: Jesus is emphasizing the folly of choosing the wrong way, the wisdom of choosing the right . . . and the impossibility of having both. It is an either-or proposition. I repeat, when we question that and attempt to travel both paths, keeping the wrong a secret, the life of simple faith erodes.

Now let's go back to Jesus' four contrasts. The first has to do with the *treasure* of our lives, which is what we have—our possessions. The rest have to do with the *focus* of our lives, which is what we are—our direction. Let's take them in that order.

Our Treasure: What We Possess

Our earthly treasure is not difficult to identify. It would include anything that is tangible and has a price tag. We can see it, touch it, measure it, and enjoy it. Our heavenly treasure would include the invisible, intangible, priceless possessions that belong to anyone who is numbered among God's forever family. The former, according to the Master, can corrode, age, deteriorate, and be ripped off. For the latter, however, none of that is true.

Exactly what is it He is prohibiting when He says, "Do not lay up . . ."? Possessions in and of themselves? No. Scripture does not condemn owning possessions. How about planning for the future? Is Jesus telling us not to buy insurance and not to face the future with some sort of strategy? No. Well, then, is our Lord condemning the enjoyment of things we own, even nice things? Again, no. In spite of all you may have heard or believed, none of the above is the point Jesus is making. Matter of fact, we are distinctly told that God gives us "all things to enjoy" (1 Tim. 6:17). Yes, *enjoy.* Paul found that he not only needed to learn "to be content in whatever circumstances" he found himself, but he also needed to learn "how to live in prosperity" as well as with "humble means" (Phil. 4:11-12). I know, I know. Some have taken this prosperity issue to such an extreme that they have learned how to rationalize ostentatious opulence, clearly an incorrect and unbiblical interpretation. But equally tragic are those who have not learned how to accept or enjoy anything above the lowest economic level, believing if they do so, they will be unspiritual. Few responses are more shame-based and guilt-oriented than that. Since I have already dealt with that issue in great detail in *The Grace Awakening*, there is no need to repeat those same things here.

What, then, is Jesus denouncing? Namely this: the selfish accumulation of tangible treasure to the point where enough is never enough . . . extravagant living to the exclusion of others in need. More specifically, it's setting our hearts on earthly things so much so that we don't own them, they own us. How easy in our materialistic age to be "lured into a lesser loyalty" by fixing our attention on things that have price tags.

This is a perfect moment to stop for a quick self-analysis. I am not interested in how much you make or what choices you make regarding your lifestyle. Who am I to judge another? My concern really has nothing to do with what you own but rather with why you own it. In light of what we have just read, can you honestly say that your heart is not fixed on tangible treasures? Is your giving generous? Do you readily help others, even as you enjoy God's gracious provisions? Are you genuinely unselfish, openhanded, greathearted, free from materialistic addictions? Selfishness evidences itself in the materialist who always wants more and in the miser who hoards needlessly.

Martin Luther wrote:

> Whenever the Gospel is taught and people seek to live according to it, there are two terrible plagues that always arise: false preachers who corrupt the teaching, and then Sir Greed, who obstructs right living.[2]

I do not know of a more pronounced idol in this generation than "Sir Greed." I'm convinced it is more powerful and certainly more popular than lust, especially in these United States. If you are determined to simplify your life, you will need to ask yourself some hard questions: Why do you want that second job? Why are you working such long hours? Why have you deliberately put your family on hold while you play Russian roulette with greed? When will you be able to say,

"Enough"? Why is your occupation or your position so important to you?

Am I suggesting that if you are really a person of devotion you would leave your present occupation and go into the ministry? No way. I am just maverick enough to say that I think fewer Christians ought to be going into the ministry and more should be going into business and into occupations that have nothing to do with vocational Christian service. As I mentioned earlier, I don't see life divided into public and private, secular and sacred. It is all an open place of service before our God. My hope is to see this generation produce a group of Christians who will infiltrate our society—in fact, our entire world—with a pure, beautiful message of grace and honesty in the marketplace.

Recently I had a delightful talk with a keen-thinking young man following one of the worship services at our church. As we visited, I asked him about his future plans. "Well, I've just graduated from law school," he said. When I asked about how he hoped to use his training, he said, "I want to be a man of integrity who practices law." What refreshing words! They reflected the right priority. There is not a career worth pursuing where you *cannot* have integrity. Every vocation cries out for it.

Rather than placing all the emphasis on earthly, tangible treasures, our Lord instructs us to turn our attention to those intangible treasures that defy destruction and cannot be stolen—eternal treasures that keep the perspective clear.

Back in the spring of 1991 my wife and I were invited to Washington, D.C., as guests of the Christian Embassy. That trip proved to be one of the most eventful of our lives, as we had the opportunity to meet and spend time with some of the highest ranking officers in all the branches of our military services, many of whom are sterling Christians. I ministered to a group of them early one morning at the Pentagon. As we sat around a long table together, Bibles opened, they were anxious to hear what God's Word had to say about their lives. Though incredibly responsible, intelligent, and decisive men, they were as unassuming and teachable as schoolchildren . . . and far more attentive! Because they were men who were laying up treasures in heaven, their hearts were open and receptive.

Our trip included a visit to the Oval Office where we were privileged to meet the president and vice president—wonderful experience! We found our highest elected national leaders to be gracious and kind men. This was followed by my being given the opportunity to address a room full of greathearted people serving on the White House staff—another delightful occasion. We found these people to be teachable folks with servant hearts, not at all like the press often portrays them.

The climax of our East Coast trip occurred at a retreat center in the Blue Ridge Mountains of Virginia, a place called Wintergreen. There over one hundred

Pentagon-based officers, plus senators and representatives from Capitol Hill, had gathered for spiritual renewal. We prayed, laughed, sang, spent time in the Scriptures, and shared that slice of life together in a relaxed setting. Most of these people had played significant roles in the Vietnam War as well as the victorious war in the Persian Gulf; yet there they sat, drinking in the truth of Scripture, grateful for a chance to receive insights from God's eternal and inerrant Word. As Cynthia and I flew back to California, though exhausted from our five-day investment of time and energy, we were over-flowing with gratitude. We had been with those who had every earthly reason to be full of pride and/or cynicism, but were neither. They had discovered over the years that the teachings of Christ were more significant than anything they dealt with professionally . . . and that glorifying Him was far more important than fighting wars or pleasing the public. Their hearts were right, therefore their treasures were in correct perspective. Putting together a strategy that would result in a successful military campaign was, of course, important, but not more important than their simple faith in God's dear Son.

Our Focus: What We Are

Let's take another look at Jesus' words here:

The lamp of the body is the eye; if therefore your eye is

clear, your whole body will be full of light. But if your eye
is bad, your whole body will be full of darkness. If therefore the light that is in you is darkness, how great is the
darkness! No one can serve two masters; for either he will
hate the one and love the other, or he will hold to one and
despise the other. You cannot serve God and mammon.

Matthew 6:22-24

Jesus uses an illustration from basic human anatomy
to illustrate the importance of the right focus in life.
Just as the eye affects our whole body ("the lamp of the
body is the eye"), so our focus (whatever we set our
hearts on) impacts our whole life. Paul, a few years
later, put it this way:

If then you have been raised up with Christ, keep seeking the things above, where Christ is, seated at the right
hand of God. Set your mind on the things above, not on
the things that are on earth. For you have died and your
life is hidden with Christ in God.   Colossians 3:1-3

Finally, brethren, whatever is true, whatever is honor-
able, whatever is right, whatever is pure, whatever is
lovely, whatever is of good repute, if there is any excel-
lence and if anything worthy of praise, let your mind
dwell on these things.   Philippians 4:8

Clearly, our minds determine the direction of our
lives. Whatever we think on, we become. Right focus–
good results; wrong focus–bad results. Or, as Christ
describes it, clear eyes–light; bad eyes–"how great is

the darkness!" In other words, "How far you can be lured from the right loyalty . . . how confused you can become, simply by false focus!" We can, in fact, be enslaved by the wrong master. Remember His words— "No one can serve two masters."

D. Martyn Lloyd-Jones, in his splendid work on the Sermon on the Mount, titles the chapter in which he addresses these words of Jesus, "Sin's Foul Bondage." And so it is. The "great darkness" that accompanies an out-of-focus life is nothing less than the foul bondage brought on by sin.

> According to the Scripture man was made in the image of God; and a part of the image of God in man is undoubtedly the mind, the ability to think and to reason, especially in the highest sense and in a spiritual sense. Man, therefore, was obviously meant to function in the following way. His mind, being the highest faculty and propensity that he possesses, should always come first. Things are perceived with the mind and analysed by it. Then come the affections, the heart, the feeling, the sensibility given to man by God. Then thirdly there is that other quality, that other faculty, called the will, the power by which we put into operation the things we have understood, the things we have desired as the result of apprehension.[3]

During the days of our innocence (that is, Adam's and Eve's innocence), things were in proper order. There was the mind, which gave facts to the body and prompted the emotions to respond correctly. In turn, the emotions signaled the will, which carried out the desires, and obedience followed. The mind learned, based upon the facts of truth, then dictated to the emotions the proper response, which gave the will the green light to move ahead and obey. When "sin's foul bondage" occurred (when Adam and Eve fell into sin in the Garden), the first two were reversed. The tragedy is this: We still live like that. Now what is considered of foremost importance is what "feels good."

D. Martyn Lloyd-Jones then defines the tragic results of sin in four ways.

- Sin causes an entire disturbance to the normal function.

- Sin blinds us in certain vital respects.

- Sin makes us a slave of the things that were originally meant to serve us. (The thing that would shock us and keep us from sin, the addiction of the thing, becomes our *drive*. And it is indeed an addiction.)

- Sin entirely ruins us.[4]

I have talked with individuals whose focus has gotten out of whack, and I have attempted to dissuade them on the basis of sheer logic, basic facts, evidence, scriptural truth—the whole nine yards. They may listen, but when I am through, it is like a stiff arm extends in my direction, saying, "Don't bother me. I know what

I'm doing." What they are doing is serving the wrong master. And their addiction has blinded them. Returning to Jesus' closing words, we can understand His reason for saying:

> No one can serve two masters; for either he will hate the one and love the other, or he will hold to one and despise the other. You cannot serve God and mammon.   Matthew 6:24

You cannot! Let those words sink in. You cannot be a slave of two masters simultaneously. It cannot occur. When wrongly enslaved, simple faith erodes, which explains why Paul wrote so passionately to the Corinthians:

> But I am afraid, lest as the serpent deceived Eve by his craftiness, your minds should be led astray from the simplicity and purity of devotion to Christ.
> Corinthians 11:3

A mind that is "led astray from the simplicity . . . of Christ" is one whose loyalty has been divided. When that happens, erosion has been set in motion.

SIMPLY PUT: THE SECURITY OF LIVING IN TRUTH

I have given a lot of thought to these things, not only because I have tried to figure out why some who once walked in "simplicity and purity" no longer do, but also because I realize I am vulnerable to the same temptation to drift. While pondering these things, two thoughts keep coming to the surface of my mind. Let me state and explain both.

First, *by living in truth our options remain open.* The secret is making the right choices. Here's what I mean. In the light of truth, you and I are able to see both truth and lie, both light and darkness—that which is simple, pure, and clear and that which is deceptive. But enslaved to darkness and plunged into the pit of the lie, we no longer see the truth. We have no other option but to believe the lie. We become victimized in our addiction—in "sin's foul bondage."

The secret, of course, is making the right choices every day. So? Watch those choices! Watch your decisions!

No married couple suddenly divorces. No home suddenly fractures. No church suddenly splits. Nobody becomes a cynic overnight. Nobody makes one leap from the pinnacle of praise to the swamp of carnality. Erosion is a slow and silent process based on secret choices. And isn't it remarkable? If you do not stop yourself in the downward process, last week's wrong choice doesn't seem quite so bad this week. In fact, in a month's time it seems like not that bad a choice at all! Thus simple faith erodes into a life of secrecy and complication.

Second, *by living in truth, our focus stays clear.* The secret here is serving the right Master. We need to keep asking ourselves, Does this honor the Savior? Does this exalt my Lord? Does this bring glory to His name? Does this lift Him up? How powerful is our focus!

Let me level with you. I know some of you are thinking, *I'm never going to become that wicked old man. I have had enough warning, Chuck. I have heard enough sermons on this theme. I've read the Scriptures. I know the verse that says, "Let him who thinks he stands take heed lest he fall." I'm safe.* For you, especially, I close the chapter with this story.

Robert Robinson was born in England more than two hundred years ago. When he was just a boy, his father died, and his widowed mother sent him to London to learn the trade of barbering. In that great city Robert came under the persuasive influence of a powerful man of God, the great Methodist revivalist George Whitefield. Robinson was soundly converted and felt a call to the ministry; he began at once to study for a lifetime of serving Christ.

At twenty-five Robert Robinson was called to pastor a Baptist church in Cambridge, where he became very successful. But the popularity was more than the young minister could handle. It led to the beginning of a lapse in his life of simple faith. Ultimately he fell into carnality, another tragic victim of "sin's foul bondage." As the years passed he faded from the scene and few even remembered his earlier years of devotion to Christ.

Years later Robinson was making a trip by stage-coach and happened to sit next to a woman who was reading a book with obvious pleasure. She seemed to be especially interested in one page of the volume, for she kept returning to it again and again. Finally she turned to Robinson—a complete stranger to her—and held the page toward him. Pointing to the hymn she had been reading there, she asked what he thought of it.

Robinson looked at the first few lines:

> Come, Thou Fount of every blessing
> Tune my heart to sing Thy grace;
> Streams of mercy, never ceasing,
> Call for songs of loudest praise. . . .

He read no further. Turning his head, he endeavored to engage the lady's attention on the passing landscape. But she was not to be denied. Pressing her point, she told him of the benefit she had received from the words of that hymn and expressed her admiration for its message.

Overcome with emotion, Robinson burst into tears. "Madam," he said, "I am the poor, unhappy man who wrote that hymn many years ago, and I would give a thousand worlds, if I had them, to enjoy the feelings I had then."[5]

Robert Robinson was now many years older and light-years removed from his earlier commitment to Christ. His days of simple faith had eroded. How ironic that, at the end of the hymn, he had seemed to prophesy his own downward course:

> O to grace how great a debtor
> Daily I'm constrained to be!
> Let Thy goodness, like a fetter,
> Bind my wandering heart to Thee:
>
> Prone to wander, Lord, I feel it,
> Prone to leave the God I love;
> Here's my heart, O take and seal it;
> Seal it for thy courts above.[6]

That is precisely what he did. Robert Robinson died shortly thereafter at the young age of fifty-five, the victim of the lure of a lesser loyalty. He had left the God he once loved and had become "a wicked old man."

CHAPTER TEN

The Subtle Enemy of Simple Faith

OKAY, now that I have your attention, what is it? Which sin is the subtle enemy of simple faith? In the previous chapter we spent a lot of time on materialism and greed. But neither of those is the enemy I have in mind. Furthermore, neither is all that subtle. Anyone who battles either materialism or greed soon telegraphs the struggle publicly. How about anger? No, that's not it. Or lust? Wrong again. We have already taken a long look at hypocrisy, as well as several of the commandments Jesus restated having to do with murder, adultery, divorce, and making false vows, but those would not qualify as *subtle* enemies.

Stop and think. Once you decide to trust God in simple faith and allow Him complete freedom to carry out His plan and purpose in you as well as through you, you need only relax and count on Him to take care of things you once tried to keep under control. From now on you won't step in and take charge. "God is well able to handle this," you tell yourself. But in a weak moment the adversary of your soul whispers a doubt or two in your ear, like, "Hey, what if–?" If that doesn't make you churn, he returns in the middle of the night and fertilizes your imagination with several quasi-extreme possibilities, leaving you mildly disturbed if not altogether panicked. No one can tell by looking (and you certainly wouldn't think of *telling* anyone), but in place of your inward peace and simple faith, you are now immobilized by . . . what? You guessed it, the most notorious faith killer in all of life: *worry*.

A BRIEF ANALYSIS OF WORRY

> For this reason I say to you, do not be anxious for your life, as to what you shall eat, or what you shall drink; nor for your body, as to what you shall put on. Is not life more than food, and the body than clothing?   Matthew 6:25

Being something of a wordsmith, I find the term "worry" fascinating, though the reality of this in our lives can be downright maddening. To begin with, the word used by Matthew (translated here as "anxiety" and "anxious") is the Greek term *merimnao*. It is a combination of two smaller words, *merizo*, meaning "to divide," and *nous*, meaning "the mind." In other words, a person who is anxious suffers from a divided mind, leaving him or her disquieted and distracted. Actually, our English word *worry* is from the German, *worgen*, which in that tongue means "to strangle." This ties in vividly with what Jesus taught when He spoke on another occasion of the farmer who sowed good seed among thorns. When interpreting what He meant in that parable, He explained:

> And others are the ones on whom seed was sown among the thorns; these are the ones who have heard the word, and the worries of the world, and the deceitfulness of riches, and the desires for other things enter in and choke the word, and it becomes unfruitful.   Mark 4:18-19

Did you catch that? Those thornlike "worries of the world . . . choke the word," making it unfruitful. Worry strangles the good Word of God that has been sown, rendering it ineffective and making those who once walked in simple faith unproductive people.

Of all the biblical stories illustrating worry, none is more practical or clear than the one recorded in the last five verses of Luke 10. Let's briefly relive it.

Jesus dropped by His friends' home in Bethany. He was, no doubt, tired after a full day, so nothing meant more to Him than having a quiet place to relax with friends who would understand. However, Martha, one of the friends, turned the occasion into a mild frenzy. To make matters worse for her, Martha's sister Mary was so pleased to have the Lord visit their home that she sat with Him and evidenced little concern over her sister's anxiety attack.

Now as they were traveling along, He entered a certain village; and a woman named Martha welcomed Him into her home. And she had a sister called Mary, who moreover was listening to the Lord's word, seated at His feet. But Martha was distracted will all her preparations.
                                        Luke 10:38–40a

You've got the picture. To Martha, preparing a big meal was the only option ("Nothing but the best for Jesus" must have been in the back of her mind), so she became "distracted"—another colorful Greek term meaning "to draw around," like being mentally knotted up in a network of frayed emotions. We can imagine the dear lady scurrying around the kitchen, kneading dough, basting the lamb, boiling the vegetables, trying to locate her best dishes, hoping to match tablecloth and napkins, ultimately needing help to get it all ready at the proper time. We have all been there, but usually we've had a few extra hands to help. Martha didn't, and that was the final straw. Irritated, exasperated, and angry,

. . . she came up to Him, and said, "Lord, do You not care that my sister has left me to do all the serving alone? Then tell her to help me."   Luke 10:40b

Her boiling point led to blame: "Don't you even care, Lord? Tell her to get up from there and come in the kitchen and help me!" Martha was so upset that she commanded Jesus to do something about it. But

Jesus was neither impressed at her busyness nor intimidated by her command. Graciously, yet firmly, He said:

> . . . Martha, Martha, you are worried and bothered about so many things; but only a few things are necessary, really only one, for Mary has chosen the good part, which shall not be taken away from her.   Luke 10:41-42

Those two terms He used to describe her attitude are significant: *worried* and *bothered*. The first one, translated "worried," is the same term found in Matthew 6, translated "anxious" . . . *merimnao*. "Martha! You are so mentally torn, you are trying to do too many things at once"—that sort of thing. Worry occurs when we assume responsibility for things that are outside our control. And I love His solution—"only a few things are necessary, really only *one*." What a classic example of simple faith! This could very well mean "only one dish." We'd say today, "Just fix a sandwich, Martha." Martha had complicated things by turning the meal into a holiday feast. Not Mary. All Mary wanted was time with Jesus . . . and He commended her for that. Mary's simple faith, in contrast to her sister's panic, won the Savior's affirmation.

What is wrong with worry? It is incompatible with faith. They just don't mix.

How can we conquer worry? The story of Martha and Mary comes in handy here, for in it I find three helpful answers.

- *Realistic expectations.* Martha set her heart on many hopes and dreams. She was driven by idealism. Mary? Only one thing occupied her mind. She was content to sit and relax in the presence of her Lord.

- *Refusal to play God.* Martha had a game plan and she convinced herself that it was God's as well. That is why she rebuked Jesus for not cooperating. When Mary didn't move toward the kitchen, Martha assumed the role of the fourth member of the Trinity and told Jesus to get with it.

- *Remember God's character.* Is God good? Is He just? Fair? Reliable? Faithful? Worriers (like Martha) tend to forget that the Lord is imminently capable of handling *every* situation. Because He is God we can count on Him to come through.

It has been my observation that worriers are basically dissatisfied people. Something is never quite right. When one thing is fixed, something else is out of whack. Contentment with the way things are, even knowing that God could change them if He wished, is a mind-set that is foreign to the worrier. What *is* is not enjoyed because of what *could* be. Whoever chooses to live like that should be ready for a lifetime of dissatisfaction.

About a year ago I came across a piece written by fourteen-year-old Jason Lehman. Because it is such an apt description of what I'm trying to say, I will let it speak for itself.

Present Tense

It was spring
But it was summer I wanted,
The warm days,
And the great outdoors.
It was summer,
But it was fall I wanted,
The colorful leaves,
And the cool, dry air.
It was fall,
But it was winter I wanted,
The beautiful snow,
And the joy of the holiday season.
It was winter,
But it was spring I wanted,
The warmth
And the blossoming of nature.
I was a child,
But it was adulthood I wanted.
The freedom,
And the respect.
I was 20,
But it was 30 I wanted,
To be mature,
And sophisticated.
I was middle-aged,
But it was 20 I wanted,

The youth,
And the free spirit.
I was retired,
But it was middle age I wanted,
The presence of mind,
Without limitations.
My life was over.
But I never got what I wanted.[1]

JESUS' COUNSEL TO WORRIERS

I am so pleased that our Lord included the subject of worry in His message on the mountain. In fact, He devotes more space to this issue than any other. Those with keen eyes could have seen it coming. When He said, "Do not lay up for yourselves treasures upon earth," it was His way of saying, "Get your eyes off the horizontal!" And later when He warned, "You cannot serve God and mammon (money)," He was talking about living with divided objectives . . . having a "divided mind" *(meriomnao)*. So we shouldn't be surprised that He jumps right into the whole world of the worrier, a person enslaved to earthly perspectives.

I want to suggest a new outline of Matthew 6. It may seem a little elementary at first, but you won't forget it, guaranteed! You want things simple? Here's *simple!*

Matthew 6:1–18
Warning against parading our acts of righteousness
Do not brag!

Matthew 6:19–24
Warning against falling into the trap of materialism
>*Do not sag!*

Matthew 6:25–32
Warning against being preoccupied with wrong things
>*Do not worry!*

Matthew 6:33–34
Warning against anticipating all of tomorrow's concerns today
>*Do not hurry!*

Jesus' Repeated Commands

Before going any further, we need to read Jesus' words about worry. Since this marks the core of His message, let's take our time. If you are in a place where you can do so, read the paragraph aloud.

For this reason I say to you, do not be anxious for your life, as to what you shall eat, or what you shall drink; nor for your body, as to what you shall put on. Is not life more than food, and the body than clothing? Look at the birds of the air, that they do not sow, neither do they reap, nor gather into barns, and yet your heavenly Father feeds them. Are you not worth much more than they? And which of you by being anxious can add a single cubit to his life's span? And why are you anxious about clothing? Observe how the lilies of the field grow; they do not toil nor do they spin, yet I say to you that even Solomon in all his glory did not clothe himself like one of these. But if God so arrays the grass of the field, which is alive today and tomorrow is thrown into the furnace, will He not much more do so for you, O men of little faith? Do not be anxious then, saying, "What shall we eat?" or "What shall we drink?" or "With what shall we clothe ourselves?" For all these things the Gentiles eagerly seek; for your heavenly Father knows that you need all these things. But seek first His kingdom and His righteousness; and all these things shall be added to you. Therefore do not be anxious for tomorrow; for tomorrow will care for itself. Each day has enough trouble of its own.   Matthew 6:25-34

If you like to mark the book you are reading, you will want to underscore the identical commands "Do not be anxious." Each time it is *merimnao,* "do not be divided in your mind—double-minded." Elsewhere in Scripture we are told that a person who is double-minded is unstable (James 1:8). Harassed and haunted either by what we think might happen or by something that has already occurred—neither of which we can control or change—we become fearful and unsure. Most worries not only haven't happened, they won't ever happen . . . and many worry over that! They are sure the other shoe will fall, and it is maddening to wait for that to happen. If we were to keep a record of our fears for fifty years of our lives, chances are good that

90 percent (or more) of those things we dreaded never came to pass.

Clarence Macartney's story about Thomas Carlyle is a good example.

> In his house in Chelsea in London they show you the sound-proof chamber, a sort of vaulted apartment, which Carlyle had built in his house so that all the noise of the street would be shut out and he could do his work in unbroken silence. One of his neighbors, however, kept a cock that several times in the night and in the early morning gave way to vigorous self-expression. When Carlyle protested to the owner of the cock, the man pointed out to him that the cock crowed only three times in the night, and that after all that could not be such a terrible annoyance. "But," Carlyle said to him, "If you only knew what I suffer waiting for that cock to crow!"[2]

Again and again our Lord admonishes His people who wish to live lives of simple faith, "Do not be anxious!" This is not a series of mild suggestions, understand . . . but *commands*. Do not! In other words, stop it!

Pay attention to the three areas He identifies:

- Do not be anxious for your *life* (v. 25)
- Do not be anxious for your *needs* (v. 31)

    "What shall we eat, drink, wear?" Charles Spurgeon called these "the world's trinity of care."

- Do not be anxious for *tomorrow* (v. 34)

  "A mild recession is sure to come."

  "The unemployment rate will certainly rise."

  "The housing market is due to take a hit."

  "Money will be tight next year."

  "A huge earthquake—the big one—will probably hit this area within the next six months . . . certainly not more than nine months from now."

My family and I have been living in Southern California since the summer of 1971. Do you know how long we have heard doomsday warnings about "the big one"? *Since the summer of 1971.* Am I saying we should not be prepared? No, of course not. Never once did Jesus advocate an irresponsible or careless lifestyle. But worry? That is, live out our lives every day distracted by the dread of a possible quake that may reach 8.5 on the Richter scale? What good would *that* do? Think of all the energy I would have expended and all the time I would have wasted since 1971. Furthermore, think of what such hopeless dread would have done to my mind . . . and what a heavy toll it would have taken on my leadership. Worry is not only incompatible with faith, it also siphons hope from our hearts . . . and hope is our main fuel for the future. Take away hope and it is curtains.

Years ago an S-4 submarine was rammed by a ship off the coast of Massachusetts and sank immediately. The entire crew was trapped in a prison house of death. Every effort was made to rescue them but all failed. Near the end of the ordeal, a diver placed his helmeted ear to the side of the vessel and heard a tapping from inside. He recognized it as Morse Code. It was a question, forming slowly: "Is . . . there . . . any . . . hope?"[3]

If I may hitchhike on that true story, let's let the sub represent life and let's pretend we are the ones trapped inside. If Jesus were the diver, He would tap back: "Do . . . not . . . be . . . anxious . . . I . . . am . . . in . . . full . . . control."

Jesus' Penetrating Questions

Jesus' sermon does not provide the answers to all our questions, but it does address some of our most crucial questions. As I read through and ponder Jesus' statements, no fewer than five questions leap off the page:

- Isn't life more than food and the body more than clothing? The anticipated answer is "Yes, of course."

- After mentioning the tiny birds of the air and how faithfully the Father feeds them, another probing question occurs: Aren't you worth much more than they? Again, the clear implication:

"Absolutely!"

- Then He asks a question regarding the ineffec-
tiveness, the complete waste, of worry. Which of
you by worrying about it can add even one inch
to your height? (Or one day to your life?) Now
there's something to think about!

- The fourth question strikes at the issue of
motive: Why are you worried about what you
wear? Those why questions—they *really* penetrate, don't they?

- The last question forces us to think
theologically . . . and rare are those who do.
Won't God do much more for you than He does,
say, for the field lilies or the grass that grows wild
in the meadow?

These five questions touch the tender nerve endings
of our lives. They probe our temporal desires, our
worth in God's estimation, our hidden motives, our
theology, our perspective.

To live in simple faith is not to practice a head-in-
the-sand theology. None of what I write is intended to
suggest that we stop thinking and drift into
Fantasyland, expecting God to cook our meals, set the
table, serve the food, and do the dishes, while all we do
is sit and eat. As responsible and thinking believers,
we are to be engaged in the demands of everyday

living . . . but free of the accompanying worry that plagues the pagans who have no God.

Jesus' Vivid Illustrations

While we are dissecting the sermon Jesus preached, two illustrations stand out in bold relief.

First, *when it comes to food*, "look at the birds of the air." Maybe a couple of Palestinian sparrows flitted by just then and He looked up and pointed in their direction. He carries it further by mentioning that those tiny rascals don't plant seed, neither do they harvest the crops nor store them in the barn. We have never seen a flock of "sparrow sharecroppers," yet they don't go hungry. He drives home His point by reminding everyone that those He created in His image are "worth much more" than those tiny creatures of the sky. As the old gospel song goes, "His eye is on the sparrow, and I know He watches me."

And while we are on the subject, this is a good time to allow our imagination to run free and compare the natural world to our material lives.

- No bird ever tried to build more nests or more extravagant places to live than its neighbor.

- No fox ever got ticked off because she had only one hole in which to hide and rear her young.

- No squirrel ever had a coronary because he failed

to store enough nuts for two winters instead of one.

- No bear was ever envious of another bear with a larger cave in which to hibernate.

- No dog ever lost a good night's sleep over the fact that he had not laid aside enough bones for his declining years. And yet our heavenly Father takes wonderfully good care of all His creatures. What a waste is worry!

Second, *when it comes to clothing*, "observe how the lilies of the field grow." They don't compare or complain; they simply grow and bloom, grow and bloom, grow and bloom. Wherever they are planted, they grow . . . and whether they are appreciated or are not even noticed, they burst forth into brilliant blossoms. As Jesus put it, not even Solomon at the height of his prosperous career wore kingly robes or jeweled crowns more beautiful than the lilies that adorned the landscape surrounding his palace. And though his resplendent residences housed more anxiety and heartaches than we can imagine, those lilies outside grew and bloomed free of both.

From the tiny birds of the air and from the fragile lilies of the field we learn the same truth, which is so important for those who desire a life of simple faith: God takes care of His own. He knows our needs. He anticipates our crises. He is moved by our weaknesses. He stands ready to come to our rescue. And at just the right moment He steps in and proves Himself as our faithful heavenly Father.

SIMPLY PUT: OUR RELIEF FROM WORRY

But seek first His kingdom and His righteousness; and all these things shall be added to you. Therefore do not be anxious for tomorrow; for tomorrow will care for itself. Each day has enough trouble of its own.
Matthew 6:33–34

Do you really want to live a worry-free life? I mean, are you serious about getting rid of those mental distractions and emotional drains? If so, these concluding verses in Matthew 6 offer the two passwords for entering that new mode of existence: *priorities* and *simplicity*.

Priorities

Put first things first. Each morning as you get up to face the day, tell the Lord, "Today, my desire is to seek Your will, Lord . . . Your righteousness. Whatever happens, whatever I encounter, may I be sensitive to Your presence and depend on Your strength. May Your kingdom agenda be my top priority, the most significant thought in my mind. This day is Yours, Lord."

If I read verse 33 correctly, all the stuff you once worried about and fretted over will fall into place. As you care more and more about giving Him first priority, you will care less and less about the things that once "strangled" you emotionally and spiritually, thereby stealing your peace. Furthermore, who's to say that things are as bad as they may seem? I usually discover later on that good things were happening even when it seemed nothing was working out right.

That statement is illustrated perfectly in a story I heard recently that made me smile. It's about a farmer who wanted to breed his three sows. He had a friend who owned a few boars, so they made arrangements to get the sows and boars together. One afternoon the farmer loaded the sows into his pickup truck and hauled them over to the nearby farm. While the pigs were getting very well acquainted, he asked his friend how he would know if his pigs were pregnant.

"That's easy," said the man. "They wallow in the grass when it takes, but they wallow in the mud when it doesn't."

Early the next morning the farmer awoke, glanced out the window of his bedroom, and noticed all three sows wallowing in the mud. So he loaded them back into his pickup and took them for a second round with the boars. Next morning . . . same result. All three were wallowing in the mud. Disappointed but determined, the farmer once again took them back, hoping the third time would be the charm.

The following morning the farmer had to be away from the farm on business, so he anxiously phoned his wife, "Are they wallowing in the grass or the mud, dear?"

"Neither," she replied. "But two of them are in the back of your pickup and the third one's up front honking the horn!"

Maybe the farmer was worried about not getting his way, but the pigs were having the time of their lives. Things are seldom as bad as we think.

Simplicity

Live one day at a time. You've heard it before: Don't contaminate today by corrupting it with tomorrow's troubles. Refuse—yes, *refuse*—to allow tomorrow's lagoon of worries to drain into today's lake. Today is challenge enough! And since you will need fresh energy and new insight to handle what tomorrow throws at you, wait until it dawns before taking it on. Some of the things you do today may seem totally insignificant so far as tomorrow is concerned, but stay at it. Keep life simple. Do what you have to do today and, to your surprise, it may make an enormous difference in the world you wake up to tomorrow. And while I'm tossing out all this advice, never underestimate the importance of even the most menial of tasks you carry out each day. Don't think that some slight contribution you make on a given day is not worth the effort . . . or won't make any difference tomorrow.

In his book, *The Fall of Fortresses,* author Elmer

Bendiner tells the remarkable story of a B-17 Flying Fortress that flew a bombing mission over Germany toward the end of World War II. The bomber took several direct hits from Nazi antiaircraft guns; a few actually hit the fuel tank. Miraculously, the crippled aircraft made it back without exploding or running out of fuel.

After landing, eleven unexploded twenty millimeter shells were carefully removed from the bomber's fuel tank! Each was dismantled and examined. To everyone's amazement, all eleven were empty of explosive material. Why? How could it be? Why would the enemy fire empty shells? The mystery was solved when a small note was found inside one of the shells, handwritten in Czech. Translated, it read, "This is all we can do for you now."

A member of the Czech underground, working in a Nazi munitions factory, had deliberately omitted the explosives in at least eleven of the shells on his assembly line. Not knowing if any of his sabotage efforts would prove effective, he slipped the note into one of the shells, hoping that someone who benefited from his efforts one day might discover why.

That same person may have died wondering if the quiet work he was doing to subvert the enemy war machine would ever make any difference to the outcome of the war. Nevertheless, he pressed on, doing what little he could each day, letting the future take care of itself . . . and indeed it did. There was a Flying Fortress crew who had him to thank for their lives and their future.[4]

"Each day has enough trouble of its own," said Jesus, urging us to do today only what must be done today. Those who learn to live like that have taken a giant step toward defeating the subtle enemy of simple faith.

CHAPTER ELEVEN

If You're Serious About Simple Faith, Stop This!

SOME CHRISTIANS play a lot of indoor games. Among their favorites is one we might call "Let's Label."

Here are some ground rules for starting. Find someone who is different. He or she may look different or sound different or think different. It works real well if the person holds to different opinions and/or reacts in a different way than the "acceptable manner," which differs from your religious group. This game is especially effective if someone has a mark on his or her past record that your group considers worth discussing, even if it is over and done with, fully forgiven, and none of your business (which is true over 95 percent of the time).

Here is how you play Let's Label. It involves at least six steps.

- *First step:* Find something you don't like about the person. That's not hard to do since most

people are much more demanding of others than
of themselves.

- *Second step:* Examine the externals. You have to
  do this since there is no way to know the
  "internals."

- *Third step:* Form negative and critical opinions.

- *Fourth step:* Jump to several inaccurate conclusions. This follows naturally, because there is
  always an inability to know *all* the facts.

- *Fifth step:* Mentally stick a label on the person in
  question. That saves time . . . keeps you from
  having to verify all the details.

- *Sixth step:* Freely share all findings and identifying labels with others . . . so everyone can
  "pray more intelligently."

Actually, there is another name for the game. It
doesn't sound nearly as nice or inviting, but it is the
term Jesus used in His mountain message: *judging.*

JUDGING: A QUICK 'N' DIRTY ANALYSIS

Interested in cultivating people of simple faith, Jesus
gave instructions that would help make that happen.
He cut no corners. With the skill of a surgeon, He
sliced near sensitive nerves to reach precise areas of
the heart for the purpose of doing His corrective work.

Occasionally, as we have seen already, He came across tumors that needed to be excised. When He did, He exposed them in all their ugliness. He was neither diplomatic nor sympathetic. It was His way of saying, "If you are serious about simple faith, this *has* to go!" In this case He said, "Stop it!"

What is so bad about judging? And why would Jesus have reserved some of the strongest words in His sermon for this? Four answers come to mind:

- We never know all the facts.
- We are unable to read another's motive.
- We are prejudiced people, never completely objective.
- We put ourselves in a position we are not qualified to fill . . . namely, we play God.

Most of us are so unaware of these things that we overlook our limitations. We *think* we know more than we do, hence our judging continues out of habit. Because of this we jump to false conclusions.

In one of the first books I wrote, I told a true story that's an example of this. I repeat it here because it shows how easily we could incorrectly judge another by not knowing all the facts.

A close friend of mine has an acquaintance who is a young attorney in a sizable Texas law firm. The head of this firm is a rather traditional kind of boss who enjoys a special kind of ritual at Thanksgiving time.

On the large walnut table in the boardroom of the office suite he sets out a row of turkeys, one for each member in the firm. At which point the members go through a rather involved ceremony.

Each man, in turn, steps forward and picks up the bird, announcing how grateful he is to work for the firm and how thankful he is for the turkey this Thanksgiving.

Now the young attorney is single, lives alone, and has absolutely no use for a huge turkey. But because it is expected of him, he takes a turkey every year.

One year his close friends in the law office replaced his turkey with one made of papier-mâché. They weighted it with lead to make it feel genuine, and wrapped it up like the real thing.

On the Wednesday before Thanksgiving, everyone gathered in the boardroom as usual. When it came his turn, the young attorney stepped up, picked up the large package, and announced his gratitude for the job and for the turkey.

Later that afternoon, he sat on the bus going home, the big turkey on his lap, wondering what in the world he would do with it. A little further down the bus line, a rather discouraged-looking man got on and took the vacant seat beside the young attorney.

The two men began to chat about the upcoming holiday. The lawyer learned that the stranger had spent the entire day job-hunting with no luck, that he had a large family, and that he was wondering what he would do about Thanksgiving tomorrow.

The attorney was struck with a brilliant idea: *This is my day for a good turn. I'll give him my turkey!*

Then he had second thoughts, *This man is not a free-loader. He's no bum. It would probably injure his pride for me to give it to him. I'll sell it to him.*

"How much money do you have?" he asked the man.

"Oh, a couple of dollars and a few cents," the man said.

"Tell you what. For that, I'll sell you this turkey," he said, indicating the package on his lap.

"Sold!" The stranger handed over the two dollars and a few coins. He was moved to tears, thrilled to death that his family would have a turkey for Thanksgiving.

"God bless you," he said as he got off the bus and waved goodbye. "Have a wonderful Thanksgiving. I'll never forget you."

The next Monday when the attorney got to work his friends were dying to know his reaction to the turkey. You cannot imagine their chagrin when he told them about the man on the bus—or when they told him what was really in that package. I understand, through my friend, that they all got on the bus every day that week, looking in vain for a man who, as far as I know, to this day still thinks a guy intentionally sold him a fake turkey for his last couple of bucks and some loose change.[1]

We can be certain of this: That man judged the young lawyer . . . and when you stop to analyze why, all four of the reasons I mentioned earlier apply. He didn't know all the facts, he didn't know the young man's motive, he couldn't be totally objective, and therefore he was not qualified to be the man's judge.

Enough of our own observations and analysis. It is time to see what Jesus taught.

> Do not judge lest you be judged. For in the way you judge, you will be judged; and by your standard of measure, it will be measured to you. And why do you look at the speck that is in your brother's eye, but do not notice the log that is in your own eye? Or how can you say to your brother, "Let me take the speck out of your eye," and behold, the log is in your own eye? You hypocrite, first take the log out of your own eye, and then you will see clearly to take the speck out of your brother's eye.   Matthew 7:1–5

His opening comment is a strong imperative. In essence He is saying, "Stop this!" When He says, "Do not judge!" He leaves no wobble room. He didn't intend to.

Understanding the Command

It will help us to understand what Jesus means (and does not mean) by *judge*. The term *to judge* in Greek is *krino,* which really means "to separate," but it has a much broader range of possibilities. It is a term from the ancient courtroom where a judge separated the facts and discerned or decided the truth. Occasionally the judge came to his conclusion and condemned the person on trial.

Obviously, Jesus is not telling His followers to stop being people of discernment. Throughout His mountain message He has been encouraging discernment as it relates to the scribes and Pharisees . . . and He will soon warn them to "beware of the false prophets, who come to you in sheep's clothing." Elsewhere in Scripture we are admonished, "do not believe every spirit, but test the spirits to see whether they are from God" (1 John 4:1). Some judging is not only acceptable, it is mandated. We are never to suspend our critical faculties or turn a deaf ear or close our eyes to error. Few things will remove us from a walk of simple faith quicker than putting our discernment in neutral. A gullible spirit quickly leads to complications.

What, then, does His command mean? He is saying, "Do not be censorious . . . don't conduct your life with a judgmental or negative attitude." In that sense, *to judge* means:

- to assess others suspiciously,
- to find petty faults,
- to seek out periodic weaknesses and failures,
- to cultivate a destructive and condemning spirit,
- to presume a position of authority over another.

When we do these things, we have assumed an all-knowing role that suggests we are Lord and others are our servants—a position of enormous arrogance. Paul mentioned this practice to both the Roman and Corinthian believers:

> Who are you to judge the servant of another? To his own master he stands or falls; and stand he will, for the Lord is able to make him stand. . . . But you, why do you judge your brother? Or you again, why do you regard your brother with contempt? For we shall all stand before the judgment seat of God. For it is written,
>
> > "AS I LIVE, SAYS THE LORD, EVERY KNEE SHALL BOW TO ME,
> >   AND EVERY TONGUE SHALL GIVE PRAISE TO GOD."
>
> So then each one of us shall give account of himself to God.
>
> Therefore let us not judge one another anymore, but rather determine this—not to put an obstacle or a stumbling block in a brother's way.   Romans 14:4, 10-13

> For I am conscious of nothing against myself, yet I am not by this acquitted; but the one who examines me is the Lord. Therefore do not go on passing judgment before the time, but wait until the Lord comes who will both bring to light the things hidden in the darkness and disclose the motives of men's hearts;

and then each man's praise will come to him from God.   Corinthians 4:4-5

No human—no matter how gifted or influential—is anywhere near Almighty God, possessing His omniscience and insight. The ability to read another's heart or correctly analyze all that goes into another's actions belongs to God, and to Him alone. When we act in that capacity, usurping the prerogative reserved for the Divine Judge, we play more than Let's Label; we play God. The right to give the final word about our neighbor has been denied us. Clearly, our Lord commands: "Condemn not!"

I have heard some people justify their judgmental attitude by rationalizing, "I'm not judging, I'm just inspecting fruit," which is no excuse. It is the "inspecting" part that Jesus attacks. More often than not, judging is an ego trip, prompted by pride. There are more than enough critics roaming the landscape. What we need to remember is the demoralizing impact judging has on individuals, especially those who struggle with a tender, fragile conscience. How much more wholesome and needed is a word of affirmation! William Barclay wrote that the early rabbis declared:

> There were six great works which brought a man credit in this world and profit in the world to come—study, visiting the sick, hospitality, devotion in prayer, the education of children in the Law, and *thinking the best of other people.*"[2]

That list, though old, is not a bad one to follow today.

Explaining the Reasons

As we meditate on Jesus' words, it soon becomes evi-
dent that He had reasons for such a strong command.
To begin with, the attitude we demonstrate will be the
one that returns to us. If we are good at verdicts and
sentences against others, the same will return to us. If
we pose as another's judge and jury, we cannot later
plead that we are free of the standard we administered.
If, however, we are greathearted and tolerant, forgiving and generous, we can expect the same to come
back in our direction. As Jesus said elsewhere,

> Be merciful, just as your Father is merciful. And do not
> judge and you will not be judged; and do not condemn,
> and you will not be condemned; pardon, and you will be
> pardoned. Give, and it will be given to you; good mea-
> sure, pressed down, shaken together, running over, they
> will pour into your lap. For by your standard of measure it
> will be measured to you in return.   Luke 6:36–38

A second reason is that judging is hypocritical. To
live a life of censorious suspicion filled with a condemning attitude is to choose the most hypocritical of
all lifestyles. Why? Because it implies that the critic is
free of similar (or the very same!) faults.

To communicate how ridiculous it is to operate as
though the critic is above the possibility of wrong in his

or her own life, Jesus chooses an illustration that is deliberately ludicrous and humorous: the speck-and-log analogy. Let's glance over it again:

> And why do you look at the speck that is in your brother's eye, but do not notice the log that is in your own eye? Or how can you say to your brother, "Let me take the speck out of your eye", and behold, the log is in your own eye? You hypocrite, first take the log out of your own eye, and then you will see clearly to take the speck out of your brother's eye.   Matthew 7:3–5

Dr. James Moffatt, in his translation of the New Testament, calls this the splinter-and-the-plank syndrome. The whole idea is hilarious on purpose. It doesn't take long for the imagination to run wild! Here's a guy, puffed up in self-inflated arrogance, with a "plank" protruding from his own eyeball (which he completely ignores) as he comes up close to another and engages in "splinter inspection." No wonder Jesus pulls no punches. "You hypocrite!" He says.

Charles Spurgeon captures the essence of Jesus' warning:

> Fancy a man with a beam in his eye pretending to deal with so tender a part as the eye of another, and attempting to remove so tiny a thing as a mote of splinter! Is he not a hypocrite to pretend to be so concerned about other men's eyes, and yet he never attends to his own? . . . Sin we may rebuke, but not if we indulge it. We may protest against evil, but not if we willfully

practice it. The Pharisees were great at censuring, but slow at amending.[3]

Understand our Lord's point, but don't misread it. He is not saying it is wrong to help someone deal with a "speck" that needs attention. What is hypocritical is to do so while denying the log(s) in one's own life. Only people who keep short accounts of their own failures, sins, and weaknesses have earned the right to assist others with those things in their lives. Vulnerable, humble, transparent individuals make the best confronters.

Most folks know the tragic failure of David with Bathsheba, the darkest spot on the man's record. Many, however, are not familiar with how he was confronted by Nathan the prophet. Apparently no one had said a word to David about his sin before that fateful day. When the king and the prophet finally stood nose to nose, Nathan framed his concern in an imaginary story about a man who possessed numerous sheep but who still took the one little ewe lamb that was owned by another. Nathan then posed the question: What should be done about this?

David, unaware that the story was a parable of his own careless and carnal life, spoke words of righteous-sounding anger against the man who would take advantage of another like that. There stood the hypocritical monarch, with "planks" of deception and murder in his own eye, speaking with arrogant zeal and false piety—to which Nathan replied, "You are the man!" I have no doubt that at that moment tears rushed from King David's eyes as planks and logs washed away in a flood of humiliation, allowing him to see himself clearly.

Applying the Reproof

Before proceeding, pause and ponder the depth of our Lord's words regarding a judgmental spirit. Let's face it, most Christians may not openly cheat on their mates or carry a flask of hard liquor in their pocket or double up their fists and punch another's lights out, but we will hardly hesitate to speak judgmentally of a brother or sister in God's family. Strangely, we have placed that practice in the same category of "acceptable sins" as gluttony, worry, indifference, and sloth. In the swirl of such compromise, the life of simple faith gets lost.

Just in case you find yourself rebuked by Jesus' reproof, take the time to read His half-brother's lament. Referring to the strongest muscle in our body, the tongue, James writes:

> With it we bless our Lord and Father; and with it we curse men, who have been made in the likeness of God; from the same mouth come both blessing and cursing. My brethren, these things ought not to be this way.   James 3:9-10

Do not speak against one another, brethren. He who speaks against a brother, or judges his brother, speaks against the law, and judges the law; but if you judge the law, you are not a doer of the law, but a judge of it. There is only one Lawgiver and Judge, the One who is able to save and to destroy; but who are you who judge your neighbor?   James 4:11-12

The fact is, God may wish to use us to "take the speck out of our brother's eye." If so, it is extremely important that we do so correctly.

First: We must be sure our own hands (and heart) are clean.

Second: We must be tender and gentle. We are dealing with a sensitive issue here. We are working with specks in eyes, not rocks in shoes or burrs on Levi's. Paul, the Apostle of Grace, put it this way:

Brethren, even if a man is caught in any trespass, you who are spiritual, restore such a one in a spirit of gentleness; each one looking to yourself, lest you too be tempted. Bear one another's burdens, and thus fulfill the law of Christ.   Galatians 6:1-2

I particularly like the counsel of Chrysostom: "Correct him, but not as a foe nor as an adversary exacting a penalty, but as a physician providing medicines."

Third: We must remember we are dealing with family members . . . our own brothers and sisters. They, like we, have enough people condemning, judging, and labeling them. What is really needed is tenderness and honesty mixed with compassion. What we are dealing with, bottom line, is an attitude, isn't it? Those who need help with their "specks" may be overwhelmed and blinded by their sin, but they still have feelings. They can tell immediately if we are coming to them in a spirit of gentleness or judgment. Simple faith and a sensitive spirit go hand in hand.

Very few people fully know the strength of another person's temptations. Those with mild and easily restrained temperaments cannot understand the struggles of one whose blood is afire and whose passions are controlled by a hair trigger. Those whose worlds have been protected and secure can scarcely imagine the harsh realities of life on the street. And those who have been blessed with loving, wise, and faithful parents know nothing of the temptations and battles endured by those from dysfunctional, abusive homes fractured by brutality, crime, and divorce. So? So have a heart. Apply a little grace. Correction . . . a lot of grace. Those who hope to minister deeply in others' lives must control and ultimately conquer the habit of judging fellow believers.

SIMPLY PUT: CONQUERING THE HABIT

Playing the Let's Label game can be addictive. In fact, judging can become such a habit we hardly know we are doing it. But that neither excuses it nor removes the consequences. What is needed most of all is that we stop it! The beast within us must be conquered. Here are four suggestions that may help you as much as they have helped me.

First: *Examine yourself before being tempted to inspect others.* Focus on your own areas of weakness and error. For starters, look at your own impatience, laziness, pride, intolerance, greed, lust, ingratitude, anger, careless tongue, indifference, gluttony, pessimism, and worry, to name only a few. Self-examination does wonders when we are tempted to find fault.

Second: *Confess your faults before confronting another.* I cannot explain why, but there is something therapeutic about admitting one's own weaknesses prior to facing someone you need to confront. It brings humility to the surface, sending pride to the pit . . . and humble, gentle confronters are the best confronters.

Third: *Try to understand the other person's struggle.* That will make you gentle rather than harsh and condemning. Want a helpful tip? Start at home. If you can resolve the log-and-speck tension there, you are qualified to do so elsewhere.

Fourth: *Remember, the goal is restoration, not probation.* We are to relieve a person's burden, not add to it. I wish there were a support group in every church called "Gossips Anonymous." It would be a great place for folks to go who cannot control the urge to judge . . . to malign . . . to put labels on those they criticize. Unfortunately, because Gossips Anonymous does not exist, self-appointed judges continue to run free, ignoring Jesus' command and making life miserable for many in their own spiritual family, which is really God's family. The pain they create is intense.

While I was awaiting my plane yesterday morning, a woman walked up and asked if I happened to be an author . . . the one who wrote *The Grace Awakening*. When I admitted I was the one, she very graciously expressed how thankful she was for the book, which, she said, played a part in saving her life as well as her marriage.

She had been reared in an extremely legalistic home and fell into the clutches of that negativistic, grace-killing lifestyle. The man she married became a preacher in the same religious system: long lists of taboos, exceedingly rigid expectations, unending requirements, judgmental suspicions—the works. They had a house full of children . . . and as time passed, she began to realize the collision course she and her entire family were on. She became increasingly discouraged, depressed, and overwhelmed. She could no longer ignore what all of this was doing to her husband, their children, *herself.*

Finally, she told her husband that she could not continue to live like that. The judging, the guilt, the blame, the shame-based religion . . . the whole scene was like a concentration camp from which she longed to escape. Enough was never enough. The legalism was killing the tiny bit of joy that still existed in her life. The growing hypocrisy left her even more guilty and defeated.

Courageously her husband, too, admitted many of the same feelings. Even though he knew that his career was on the line, he determined not to continue living a lie and promoting such a graceless and condemning message. Finally he resigned. My book proved helpful in the process of their change, she told me. I won't go into detail about that. Suffice it to say they quietly and bravely walked out of a dark, heavy, cultlike church setting and stepped into the sunlight of a whole new realm of grace-oriented freedom.

Their joy is returning. Their marriage has been restored. They have found a wonderful church that teaches the Scriptures and is full of encouragement, edification, genuine worship, and a balanced message of hope and obedience based on the Word of God and the life Jesus taught and modeled. The difference is that now their obedience is spontaneous, their love for God is genuine, and their relationship with others is free of binding legalism. She is virtually a new woman. Her husband is happily employed and continuing to grow in grace and the knowledge of Christ. He hopes to return to ministry as that door opens in the future.

Only one part of their story brings sadness. All their former church friends and even members of their own families have written them off. Though I felt I knew what she would say, I asked how their former friends viewed them.

She sighed, "Well, they have labeled us liberals, even though we are not that at all. Actually, we are walking closer to Christ than ever before."

I asked how it made her feel.

"In many ways we expected it," she replied. "For most of my life that is the way I handled anyone who did not agree with me. My husband and I judged them, plain and simple. We were right, and whoever was not in our group was wrong. Those are the rules of legalism."

The game goes on. Let's Label is still a favorite among many who call themselves followers of Christ. Judging continues in the name of Jesus, even though He is the One who commanded that we stop it.

CHAPTER TWELVE

The Most Powerful of All
Four-Letter Words

A WORD FITLY spoken," wrote the wise Solomon, "is like apples of gold in pictures of silver" (Prov. 25:11, KJV). Like Jell-O, concepts assume the mold of the words into which they are poured. Who has not been stabbed awake by the use of a particular word . . . or combinations of words? Who has not found relief from a well-timed word spoken at the precise moment of need? Who has not been crushed beneath the weight of an ill-chosen word? And who has not gathered fresh courage because a word of hope penetrated the fog of self-doubt? The word *word* remains the most powerful of all four-letter words.

Colors fade.

Shorelines erode.

Temples crumble.

Empires fall.
But "a word fitly spoken" endures.

Fitly spoken words are *right* words . . . the precise
words needed for the occasion. Mark Twain, a unique
wordsmith, once wrote, "The difference between the
right word and almost the right word is the difference
between lightning and lightning bug." And what power
those "right words" contain! Some punch like a jab to
the jaw, others comfort like a down pillow, still others
threaten like the cold, steel barrel of a .38 Smith and
Wesson. One set of words purifies our thoughts, trans-
planting us, at least for an instant, to the throne room
of God; another set of words ignites lust, tempting us
to visit the house of a harlot. Some words bring tears to
our eyes in a matter of seconds; others bring fear that
makes the hair on the back of our necks stand on end.

Returning momentarily to the pen of David's
greater son, we find ourselves smiling one moment
and frowning the next:

> As a ring of gold in a swine's snout,
>   So is a beautiful woman who lacks discretion.
> >   Proverbs 11:22

> When you sit down to dine with a ruler,
> Consider carefully what is before you;
> And put a knife to your throat,
> If you are a man of great appetite.
> >   Proverbs 23:1-2

Like a bad tooth and an unsteady foot
Is confidence in a faithless man in time of trouble.

Proverbs 25:19

Did such power-packed verbal missiles just flash into Solomon's mind or was he on a quest for them? He answers that question in his autobiography, in which he calls himself, "the Preacher."

In addition to being a wise man, the Preacher also taught the people knowledge; and he pondered, searched out and arranged many proverbs. The Preacher sought to find delightful words and to write words of truth correctly.

The words of wise men are like goads, and masters of these collections are like well-driven nails; they are given by one Shepherd.   Ecclesiastes 12:9-11

I love that! The man deliberately sought out "delightful" words (the Hebrew here is colorful: words that find favor, are easily grasped, readily digested), knowing that they are like "goads" (prodding, pushing us on) and "well-driven nails." Beautiful . . . and so true. J. B. Phillips has correctly assessed the impact of such words:

If . . . words are to enter men's hearts and bear fruit, they must be the right words shaped cunningly to pass men's defenses and explode silently and effectually within their minds.[1]

The finest examples of that, I repeat, are the words and phrases of Jesus Christ—His choice of words, His placement of words, His economy of words, even His eloquent turn of a phrase. Never once retreating from His all-out assault against the scribes and Pharisees, He reserved His sharpest goads for them. I am thinking of the time He took them on before His disciples and many followers, a scene recorded in Matthew 23. Seven times He blistered them with words of condemnation by repeating, "Woe to you, scribes and Pharisees, hypocrites!" (vv. 13, 14, 15, 23, 25, 27, 29). Once He called them "blind guides" (23:16) and even said they were "like whitewashed tombs" (23:27) and "serpents . . . brood of vipers" (23:33). Just picture that: "You snakes!" He said. No one ever goaded like the Son of God, hence no one's words ever penetrated like His either. Every time I hear someone in a speech refer to Jesus as if He were some kind of meek 'n' mild, spineless wimp, I want to raise my hand and ask, "Ever read Matthew 23?"

THE POWER OF JESUS' PENETRATING PRINCIPLES

Let's keep all this in mind as we get back to His message delivered from the mountain.

Dogs, Pearls, and Pigs

Do not give what is holy to dogs, and do not throw your pearls before swine, lest they trample them under their feet, and turn and tear you to pieces. Matthew 7:6

Talk about shocking words! The One who earlier urged us to shake salt and shine light and not judge . . . the One who would later implore His own to take the good news to the ends of the earth here warns against giving what is sacred to "dogs" and "throwing pearls before swine."

His choice of words was designed to startle. While we are not to judge and condemn others without knowing all the facts, neither are we to be gullible fools. To borrow from Mark Twain, "the difference between the right word and almost the right word" is the difference between being people of simple faith and being simpletons. Our Lord neither extols the virtues of gullibility (there are none), nor does He wink at a lack of discernment. To walk with God in a quiet, uncomplicated manner, sharing our faith with non-Christians, in no way suggests that we keep hammering away at stony hearts and indifferent wills.

The life-changing message of Jesus Christ's death and resurrection is a treasure beyond price. While it is ours to claim and to share, we cheapen it by pressing the issue beyond sensible bounds. Face it; some individuals are impervious to spiritual riches. They are so debauched, senseless, hateful, and closed that their continued resistance and cynicism is signal enough to encourage the discerning to turn elsewhere. There comes a point when persisting is a waste of time and energy. To quote the prophet, "Ephraim is joined to idols; Let him alone" (Hos. 4:17). We are never to give up hope, but we are wise to move on.

All this brings us to the first of three penetrating principles implied in Jesus' words: *Discernment must temper our declaration.* I am aware that endurance and faithfulness are qualities to be modeled by God's people. No question, most of us were won over because someone didn't quit when we resisted the offer of eternal life with God through Christ. Nevertheless, Jesus is teaching here that there will be occasions when perpetually closed minds need to be left on their own. In fact, when instructing His twelve disciples, He reminded them of this principle as He released them to spread His message.

> And into whatever city or village you enter, inquire who is worthy in it; and abide there until you go away. And as you enter the house, give it your greeting. And if the house is worthy, let your greeting of peace come upon it; but if it is not worthy, let your greeting of peace return to you. And whoever does not receive you, nor heed your words, as you go out of that house or that city, shake off the dust of your feet. Truly I say to you, it will be more tolerable for the land of Sodom and Gomorrah in the day of judgment, than for that city.   Matthew 10:11–15

More than once Paul modeled the same discerning style. Because he did, the Gentiles were given the opportunity to turn to Christ.

And the next Sabbath nearly the whole city assembled to hear the word of God. But when the Jews saw the crowds, they were filled with jealousy, and began contradicting the things spoken by Paul, and were blaspheming. And Paul and Barnabas spoke out boldly and said, "It was necessary that the word of God should be spoken to you first; since you repudiate it, and judge yourselves unworthy of eternal life, behold, we are turning to the Gentiles. For thus the Lord has commanded us,

"I have placed You as a light of the Gentiles, that You should bring salvation to the end of the earth."

And when the Gentiles heard this, they began rejoicing and glorifying the word of the Lord; and as many as had been appointed to eternal life believed.   Acts 13:44-48

But when Silas and Timothy came down from Macedonia, Paul began devoting himself completely to the word, solemnly testifying to the Jews that Jesus was the Christ. And when they resisted and blasphemed, he shook out his garments and said to them, "Your blood be upon your own heads! I am clean. From now on I shall go to the Gentiles."   Acts 18:5-6

Perhaps you find the idea of turning away from those who persist in their unbelief difficult to accept. You may be working with a stubborn individual who is closed . . . but in your heart you cannot release him or her. It is possible you should not; then again, maybe you would be wise to back away and let God take full charge. There is no hard-and-fast rule on this. There does come a time, however, when it is best (to borrow from a familiar saying) to "let stubborn dogs lie." Left alone, suffering under the consequences of an unbelieving, empty lifestyle could be what the stubborn one needs.

I have discovered over the years that hostile mates are seldom persuaded by a persistent, verbal witness from their believing partners. Also, those whose lives are complicated by substance abuse often must be given assistance in finding hope beyond that addiction before they can begin to grasp the gospel message. Furthermore, some folks, like Pharaoh in Moses' day, deliberately harden their hearts and become impervious to spiritual truth. In such cases, to keep pounding away is counterproductive. Simply gather up your precious pearls and move on. The soil of some souls is too hard for planting . . . which reminds me of an old Southern expression I was raised with: "You can't get sap out of a hoe handle." There comes a time when it is purposeless to persist.

But you and I *can* continue to pray. And that is exactly what Jesus addresses next in His message.

Asking, Seeking, Knocking, and Receiving

The following may sound both familiar and simple, but they are yet another example of powerful words:

Ask, and it shall be given to you; seek, and you shall find; knock, and it shall be opened to you. For everyone who asks receives, and he who seeks finds, and to him who knocks it shall be opened.   Matthew 7:7-8

"Ask . . . seek . . . knock," three powerful, monosyllabic words, all commands, urging us not to cave in with discouragement when facing the difficult or the unknown. They are all "present imperatives" in the language in which Matthew wrote them:

"Keep on asking!"
"Keep on seeking!"
"Keep on knocking!"

The implication is, "Whatever you do, don't quit; keep it up!" In childlike innocence we are to turn to our heavenly Father and trust Him to do what we cannot. And whoever said we are to ask only once has not understood the Savior's instructions: "Keep on asking . . . seeking . . . knocking." Paul, the Apostle of Grace, later wrote, "Pray without ceasing" and demonstrated it by returning to the Lord again and yet again for relief from his "thorn in the flesh" (2 Cor. 12:7-8). This kind of earnest prayer is different from the mindless repetitions we discussed in chapter 8. "Pray without ceasing" doesn't mean to endlessly mumble a monotonous set of words that lost their meaning long ago. Let's take Jesus at His word. Let's be earnestly persistent.

Having reared four children, Cynthia and I have witnessed how our children did this very thing. If we were nearby, they asked—*and kept asking*. If we happened to be out of the room, they would seek one or both of us—*and kept seeking*. If we needed a few moments of peace and quiet, we occasionally would go to our bedroom and close the door to read or talk together. Do you think the kids gave up? You know better. They knocked . . . and knocked and knocked and *kept knocking!*

Our older daughter, Charissa, and her husband, Byron, have their hands full with their two busy little ones, Parker and Heather. Now a mother in her late twenties, Charissa made a statement that reminded me of something I had said when she was her children's age. "Dad, there are days I would enjoy just five minutes all alone and to myself . . . but it is impossible. These two are *omnipresent!*" She admitted that she slipped into her bedroom the other morning and gingerly closed the door—and *locked* it—so she might sit all alone for only a few minutes. Wouldn't you know it? Sixty seconds hadn't passed before she heard two little fists pounding away on her door: "Mom, Mom! . . . Mom, are you in there?" When she didn't answer immediately, they persisted—knock, knock, KNOCK . . . KNOCK . . . *KNOCK!*

She flung open the door and looked down into two little cherubic faces as both said in unison: "Hi!" They simply wanted to be where she was. Her heart melted.

Perhaps this is a mere sampling of the way God feels about His own children. Therefore, we are invited to persist in our quest for His presence, His assistance.

Don't miss the threefold promise that accompanies the commands. What happens when we ask and seek and knock?

- "It shall be given to you"
- "You shall find"
- "It shall be opened to you"

You wish to receive something you need? Ask! You desire to find something important? Seek! You long for a tightly sealed door to open? Knock! Simple faith calls for nothing more than that: *simple faith*. No mumbo jumbo, no voodoo, no need to bargain, beg, plead, or pay penance . . . no incantations, no secret password. Nothing but the most difficult thing for high-tech, superefficient, uptight, and overachieving souls to do. Just ask in simple faith.

The Western world is not characterized by prayer. By and large, to our unspeakable shame, even genuine Christians in the West are not characterized by prayer. Our environment loves hustle and bustle, smooth organization and powerful institutions, human self-confidence and human achievement, new opinions and novel schemes; and the church of Jesus Christ has conformed so thoroughly to this environment that it is often difficult to see how it differs in these matters from contemporary paganism. There are, of course, exceptions; but I am referring to what is characteristic. Our low spiritual ebb is directly traceable to the flickering feebleness of our prayers: "You do not have, because you do not ask." [2]

In my opinion, those last nine words (quoted from James 4:2) are among the most convicting words we will ever read, which brings us to the second penetrating principle we can draw from Jesus' words: *Persistence must characterize our prayers.* There is no place for reluctance or timidity or, for that matter, uncertainty. You have a need? Then do the simple thing (and the *best* thing!) first: Ask in simple faith.

Bread, Stones, Fish, and Snakes

Jesus concludes this section of His sermon with more words fitly spoken. As you read, feel free to smile. The words are purposely colorful, even playful:

> Or what man is there among you, when his son shall ask him for a loaf, will give him a stone? Or if he shall ask for a fish, he will not give him a snake, will he?   Matthew 7:9-10

Are you a parent? If so, you have an inside track on understanding what Jesus is getting at.

Your child is hungry and doesn't hesitate to ask you for a piece of bread, perhaps a grilled-cheese sandwich.

Would you ever go outside, look around the backyard, find a rock in the flower bed, and say, "Here, kid, munch on this"? Never! We would never consider doing that to our hungry children. If you're like me, you tend to give *more* than they request. "Let's hop in the car and go get a hamburger together."

I'll go a step further. Let's imagine that your kids really love to fish. I mean it is their all-time favorite thing to do with you when a holiday or vacation time rolls around. Would you—even in your worst moment—ever *think* of taking them to a swampy, snake-infested area, cruelly substituting something unpleasant and dangerous for their very favorite pastime? Never. You would do everything possible to provide a fishing trip they would never forget. That is just the way parents are. We may be imperfect and sinful people . . . but when one of our own really wants or needs something, we do it up right. "You're hungry? How about a burger? . . . Go fishing together? I know a great spot, son!"

Now, the clincher:

If you then, being evil, know how to give good gifts to your children, how much more shall your Father who is in heaven give what is good to those who ask Him!" Matthew 7:11

Isn't that magnificent? Our perfect Father in heaven outgives all imperfect fathers on earth . . . again and again and again.

So? So persist in your prayers! So count on your Lord to answer in the best possible manner in *His way* and in *His time*. Don't be discouraged, my friend. He is faithful and good and generous and just . . . even though we are none of the above.

Others and Us

Being the ultimate wordsmith, Jesus has saved the most significant words until the last. What you are about to read is commonly called the Golden Rule.

> Therefore, however you want people to treat you, so treat them, for this is the Law and the Prophets.
>
> Matthew 7:12

What a classic example of "apples of gold in settings of silver." That single sentence is perhaps the most universally famous statement Jesus ever made, "the Everest of Ethics," as one man put it. In some ways it is the cornerstone of true Christianity, certainly the capstone of Jesus' sermon. I appreciate the positive emphasis: Instead of saying, "Don't do this," He says, "Do this." Study the statement. More importantly, live it. If you have wondered about how to get started in a lifetime of simple faith, here it is.

The principle? *Modeling must accompany our message.* You want to be forgiven? Forgive. You need affirmation? Affirm. You feel hurt, wounded, broken, and could stand a gentle touch? Be gentle with others. You have discovered the value of tact when something sensitive needed to be addressed? Be tactful. The examples are endless. Unfortunately, models of such greathearted behavior are rare. Is it any wonder the non-Christian world looks with suspicion in our direction?

The best part of the whole principle? It is so simple. Living by the Golden Rule prevents the need for laying down an endless list of little rules and regulations to govern conduct. Just put yourself in the other person's place and think, *What is it I would need if I were him or her?* And then? *Do it.* When you do, you will fulfill the essence of "the Law and the Prophets."

SIMPLY PUT: THE GREATEST MESSAGE WE CAN DELIVER

It is time to turn the tables. Throughout the book I have been referring to Jesus' greatest message. Do you know the greatest message *we* can deliver? It is the message of Christlike character. No message on earth is more needed or more powerful.

You want to impact your family . . . your church . . . your community . . . your place of employment? You want to make a difference in the life of your mate, a family member, a friend (Christian or not), some person in the workplace? Demonstrate the characteristics of Christ. No need to drop gospel tracts from a low-flying airplane or display a bright red twenty-foot-square "Jesus Saves" flag over your house. No need to stick a fish-shaped symbol on your car or quote a lot of verses every day to your neighbor or rant and rave against all the ills of society down at city hall. Just take the distilled essence of the Christian message as contained in the words of the Golden Rule and live it out. Morning to night. Day after day. Week after week. Month in, month out. Spring, summer, fall, and winter. As the prophet Micah put it: Act justly, love mercy, and walk humbly. You will be *astounded* at the impact that kind of simple-faith lifestyle will make.

It has been said that the only Bible most folks ever read is the daily life of the Christian. If that is true, I believe the world needs a *revised version*. Our problem is not that too many of us are being ignored, it's that we are all being observed!

> You are writing a gospel, a chapter each day,
>   By deeds that you do, by words that you say.
> Men read what you write, whether faithless or true.
>   Say, what is the gospel according to you?[3]

If you think that words fitly spoken are powerful, they are nothing compared to the power of a life fitly lived.

CHAPTER THIRTEEN

Simple Yet Serious Warnings for Complicated Times

ARE AMERICANS busy? Do we have a lot of irons in the fire? Have we turned what was once a simple, quiet existence into a complicated maze of activity, a Rubic's cube of complex dilemmas? You tell me.

Every day in America . . .
- 108,000 of us move to a different home, and 18,000 move to another state.
- the United States government issues 50 more pages of regulations.
- 40 Americans turn 100, about 5,800 become 65, and 8,000 try to forget their 40th birthdays.

Every day in America . . .
- 167 businesses go bankrupt while 689 new ones start up—and 105 Americans become millionaires.

- the Smithsonian adds 2,500 things to its collections.

- Americans purchase 45,000 new automobiles and trucks, and smash up 87,000.

- 20,000 people write letters to the president.

- more than 6,300 get divorced, while 13,000 get married.

- dogs bite 11,000 citizens, including 20 mail carriers.

Every day in America . . .
- we eat 75 acres of pizza, 53 million hot dogs, 167 million eggs, 3 million gallons of ice cream, and 3,000 tons of candy. We also jog 17 million miles and burn 1.7 billion calories while we're at it.[1]

It doesn't require a Ph.D. from Princeton to assess that we are busy, busy, busy. Forever on the move, doing things, eating stuff, working, jumping, jogging, writing, marrying, divorcing, buying, biting . . . you name it, our country is doing it. And in no place in our land are people doing more of it more often than this hub of humanity where I live, Southern California. The pace is somewhere between maddening and insane. The freeways are choked with traffic, people are going or coming twenty-four hours every day . . . with no letup in sight. Faces reflect tension. The air is polluted. The earth shakes. The malls are crowded. Nerves are shot. Many of the streets are dangerous. Interestingly, the more I travel to major population centers, the more I find similar scenes everywhere around the globe, not just in California.

> This is the age
> Of the half-read page.
> And the quick hash
> And the mad dash.
> The bright night
> With the nerves tight.
> The plane hop
> And the brief stop.
> The lamp tan
> In a short span.
> The Big Shot
> In a good spot.
> And the brain strain
> And the heart pain.
> And the cat naps
> Till the spring snaps—
> And the fun's done![2]

In the two-plus decades my family and I have lived out here, I have had scores of people who reside elsewhere ask me how we can stand living in such a hotbed of activity among wall-to-wall humanity. The conversation usually runs something like this:

"Don't you get tired of all the people?"

"Yes, occasionally."

"Isn't the speed of things enough to make you want to scream?"

"Often, yes, quite frankly."

"Aren't you concerned about the impact that hurry-up lifestyle and shallow-thinking mentality might have on families in general and your own kids—and grandkids—in particular?"

"Always."

"Then, haven't you given serious consideration to getting out of there and permanently relocating on some quiet, rural, wooded piece of land by a small lake . . . free of the hassle and demands of the city?"

"Never."

"Why?"

"Because there is no place I know of in America where the all-conquering message of Christ and the life of simple faith is needed more than *here.*"

When God called the Swindolls to this sprawling metropolis, He put us smack dab in the nucleus of maximum human depravity and critical needs. When I speak and write of the truth Jesus offered and the remarkable life He modeled, the contrast is so obvious out here no one has difficulty detecting the difference. People in places like this are searching for something to ease the ache and quiet the heart, mainly to bring order out of chaos and peace in place of pain. Candidly, my wife and I cannot imagine what life would be like for us in some sleepy, slow community where people talk of things like the weather and the tide, and get all hot 'n' bothered over whether the pansies and petunias will bloom early or late in the spring. If that is the kind of stuff that turns your crank, fine. All I ask is that you not feel sorry for us because we are stuck out here in wild 'n' wooly Crazyland. We really are not stuck, we're *called.* If simple faith is put to the test anywhere, it is here! And if it passes the test here, friend, it will work *anywhere.*

In a world gone mad, full of frowning people who have lost their way, the calm, wise, and timeless truths Jesus spoke make more sense than ever. What a privilege it is to communicate them.

A SIMPLE OUTLINE

You may recall earlier in the book that I suggested a four-point outline for Jesus' great sermon:

- Out with Hypocrisy! (Matt. 5)
- Down with Performance! (Matt. 6)
- Up with Tolerance! (Matt. 7:1–5)
- On with Commitment! (Matt. 7:6–29)

Throughout His message the emphasis has continued to rest on the application of truth, not just its declaration. He wants His followers to be doers of the Word, not hearers only . . . to lift sterile, antiseptic theories from the yellowed pages of the Law and the Prophets and incarnate those precepts and principles before a world that doesn't have a clue. In effect, He is saying, "Enough of external religion!" What He pleads for is an authentic transformation of life based on what the living God has said in His Word. While scribes and Pharisees sat around splitting hairs over theological and theoretical minutia, the Son of God pressed for action, which is preaching at its best. No one walked away from that hillside discourse unsure of what to do about what had been said. The question each person then (and now) needed to answer was, "Will I do these things?" Great preaching does not stop with interpretation; exhortation always follows exposition as the preacher "stops preachin' and starts meddlin'." And that is never more obvious in Jesus' sermon than when He reaches His concluding comments.

The following words of D. Martyn Lloyd-Jones express my convictions perfectly:

Here once more we are reminded that our Lord's method must ever be the pattern and example for all preaching. That is not true preaching which fails to apply its message and its truth; nor true exposition of the Bible that is simply content to open up a passage and then stop. The truth has to be taken into the life, and it has to be lived. Exhortation and application are essential parts of preaching. We see our Lord doing that very thing here. The remainder of this seventh chapter is nothing but a great and grand application of the message of the Sermon on the Mount to the people who first heard it, and to all of us at all times who claim to be Christian.

So He proceeds now to test His listeners. He says, in effect, "My Sermon is finished. Now at once you must ask yourselves a question, 'What am I doing about this? What is my reaction? Am I to be content to fold my arms and say with so many that it is a marvellous Sermon, that it has the grandest conception of life and living that mankind has ever known—such exalted morality, such wonderful uplift—that it is the ideal life that all ought to live?'" The same applies to us. Is that our reaction? Just to praise the Sermon on the Mount? If it is, according to our Lord, He might as well never have preached it. It is not praise He desires; it is practice. The Sermon on the Mount is not to be commended, it is to be carried out.[3]

Since officially entering ministry in the early 1960s, I have continued to emphasize the application of God's truth, not merely the explanation of it. Rather than stopping with ". . . and that is what Scripture teaches," how much better to continue with ". . . and this is how it is to be applied." Happily, I have found that such an emphasis is really the only way to cope with and cut through the complicated times in which we live, including life in always-on-the-move Southern California.

A STRONG REPROOF

Christ does not ask His followers to "make a few minor adjustments" or "try a little bit harder to be religious." His words call for a radical transformation—first in thinking, next in living. He leaves no third alternative, no middle ground, when He exhorts us to decide either for or against kingdom living. He expects (and deserves) our allegiance, our obedience, our very lives. When this finally becomes a reality in anyone's life, it is absolutely remarkable how many things are simplified.

Priorities that come from Him enable us to filter out the worrisome incidentals and focus only on essentials. Others' opinions pale into insignificance as we pursue His plan. Things like geography and culture and marital status and occupation are of little importance as we discern His will and walk in it. Rather than a hodgepodge of *both-ands,* the simple teachings of Christ offer us *either-ors.* How we need them!

Speaking of that, in the concluding words of Jesus' message, we find four "paired alternatives": two paths (Matt. 7:13-14), two trees (7:15-20), two claims (7:21-23), and, as we shall see in the final chapter, two foundations (7:24-29). Each requires a choice. Either we go with Him or we walk away from Him; it is as simple as that. Simple . . . not easy.

Two Paths

Enter by the narrow gate; for the gate is wide, and the way is broad that leads to destruction, and many are those who enter by it. For the gate is small, and the way is narrow that leads to life, and few are those who find it.   Matthew 7:13-14

Let me ask you, is that difficult to understand? Compared with the philosophical meanderings of our times, including all the convoluted, abstruse opinions of various intellectuals representing a broad spectrum of human thought. Jesus' comment reads like a child's primer. And because it does, sophisticated intellectuals look down their noses and sneer. To them it lacks the mind-capturing nuances of deep thought they find stimulating. How could something as basic as a narrow gate interest broad-minded thinkers? It doesn't, quite honestly. Not if they are caught up in the quest for knowledge for knowledge's sake.

C. S. Lewis doesn't hesitate to admit as much in his stimulating autobiography, *Surprised by Joy.* He writes openly of the turning point in his own life when the wide gate and the broad way attracted him. While but a thirteen-year-old schoolboy, he found the taste of intellectualism delectable:

> I was soon (in the famous words) "altering 'I believe' to 'one does feel.'" And oh, the relief of it! . . . From the tyrannous noon of revelation I passed into the cool evening of Higher Thought, where there was nothing to be obeyed, and nothing to be believed except what was either comforting or exciting.[4]

At the risk of sounding terribly simplistic to all eggheads, let me call attention to Jesus' words regarding one's ultimate destination. To make the plain painfully clear, Jesus spoke of only two conclusions to one's earthly life.

- The wide gate/broad way leads to *destruction.*
- The small gate/narrow way leads to *life.*

The broad, wide path may seem the only way to travel; however, to do so without taking into serious account its ultimate destination is dreadfully short-sighted. All the mental stimulation and intellectual excitement of scholarship notwithstanding, if that is all there is, the end is disastrous. As Solomon the wise once wrote,

> There is a way which seems right to a man,
> But the end is the way of death.
>
> Proverbs 14:12

"Enter by the narrow gate . . . the way is narrow that leads to life." What, exactly, does that mean? Rather than relying on my own words, let's look at Christ's. Elsewhere, Jesus speaks in similar terms as He addresses the same subject of enjoying eternal life with God. "I am the door; if anyone enters through Me, he shall be saved, and shall go in and out, and find pasture." (John 10:9). Here Jesus refers to Himself as "*the* door." And in yet another context, Jesus told His disciples, "I am the way, and the truth, and the life; no one comes to the Father, but through Me" (John 14:6).

Again, don't overlook the thrice-stated definite article. Jesus is not *one* of the ways, or one among several truths, or a choice alongside others leading to life. In each case, He is *the* one and only.

Paul, a genuine intellectual who turned in simple faith to Christ, wrote, "For there is one God, and one mediator also between God and men, the man Christ Jesus" (1 Tim. 2:5). Interestingly, he also singles out Jesus Christ—not as one of several mediators, but as *the* one and only.

I take it that this means precisely what it says: If an individual hopes to spend eternity with God after death, faith in Jesus Christ's death and resurrection is the only way to make that happen. In other words, Jesus is the only option. All other alternatives are roads to destruction—broad, appealing, comfortable, popular, perhaps even logical, but *wrong*.

Going back to Jesus' sermon, the same "narrow" message could be summarized in a simple series of sentences:

- There are *only two* roads to choose—one seems easy, the other hard.

- They are entered by *only two* gates—one is broad, the other narrow.

- They are traveled by *only two* crowds—many and few.

- They end at *only two* opposite destinations—destruction and life.

I am fully aware that few facts are more unpopular or more offensive than the words I have just written. In our complicated times it is far more appealing to make easy choices and remain on neutral ground. Certainly this is true among philosophical types. Nevertheless, Jesus taught otherwise, and I would be an unfaithful messenger to fail to tell you so. If you really desire a life worth living–the kind of simple faith I have been writing about for all these pages–you need to start with Christ, placing your trust in Him and Him alone. There is no other alternative that guarantees you immediate forgiveness of sins and an eternal home in heaven.

Anyone who tells you that there are other ways to God besides Christ is misguided and falls into the category of a *false teacher*. We should not be surprised to see that Jesus warns His followers of such people next in His sermon.

Two Trees

Beware of the false prophets, who come to you in sheep's clothing, but inwardly are ravenous wolves. You will know them by their fruits. Grapes are not gathered from thorn bushes, nor figs from thistles, are they? Even so, every good tree bears good fruit; but the bad tree bears bad fruit. A good tree cannot produce bad fruit, nor can a bad tree produce good fruit. Every tree that does not bear good fruit is cut down and thrown into the fire. So then, you will know them by their fruits.　　Matthew 7:15-20

Look closely. Think clearly. We live in such complicated times that wolves look and sound like sheep. They appear merciful, they seem genuine, they look beautiful, but all that is only fleece deep. Be warned! Jesus has our good at heart when He looks beneath all the externals of deceivers and exposes them for what they are—"ravenous wolves." Believe it! The problem is, you and I can't tell by a quick glance. Counterfeit Christians, like counterfeit twenty-dollar bills, are not easily detected. It takes a trained, discerning eye.

This is a good moment for me to encourage you to be a careful student of the Scriptures and a watchful follower of spiritual (perhaps a better word would be *religious*) leaders . . . in that order. The better you come to know God's truth, the keener will be your watchfulness. When Jesus spoke of checking the fruit of another's life, He was emphasizing the importance of paying attention to what is being taught—both what is said and what is left unsaid—as well as that which is taught as it is being lived out. In the final analysis, a tree cannot hide what it is. Take a close look. Slowly and carefully taste the fruit (if you can't tell by looking), get a respected second and even third opinion, and stay on the alert.

There are many who appeal to our senses and many who plead for our loyalty—and especially for our money. Discerning disciples of Christ are not fooled by all the externals: charisma and charm (or an accent!), seminary or university education, impressive résumés, beautiful facilities, large audiences, or even public appeal in the media. All those are externals that matter little. The blossoms in the spring may be lovely, but what does the fruit taste like in the fall? What matters is what is inside . . . what is being produced. Pay attention to doctrine, character, conduct, emphases, motives (if you listen and watch long enough, you can tell), and–of primary importance–how God's inerrant Word is handled. "All doctrines must be brought to the Word of God as the standard, and that, in judging of *false prophets,* the rule of faith [i.e., Scripture] holds the chief place."[5]

The difference between the genuine and the counterfeit is always subtle, never obvious. That is why so many are fooled. No one at a local department store would be deceived if I produced a twenty-dollar bill that was oversized, yellow, and had my wife's picture in the middle. But if it were a crisp, perfectly shaped, green piece of paper that bore all the marks of currency, felt like a twenty, and looked like a twenty with that distinguished picture of Andrew Jackson in the center, many would be fooled. And in comparison to counterfeit money, religious deceivers are often much more difficult to spot.

Keep in mind the "wide gate/broad way" feel-good message being promoted by the "false prophets." One of the telltale signs of these religious deceivers is their penchant to offend no one . . . to make everyone think that, no matter what, "anything goes." They use religious-sounding terms, never get specific about heaven or hell, soften the issues regarding faith in Christ alone for salvation, deliberately bypass what they consider to be "scare words" such as sin, obedience, wrong, doctrine, and repent, and promote the message that we are all in the family of God . . . regardless. Just believe, they say—it doesn't matter what you believe. Just be sincere. Just love, love, love. As a friend of mine who was saved out of that kind of nonsense said, "Those folks would have loved me right into hell."

Many years ago I was invited to attend a church with the family of a young man I had met in the Marine Corps. We drove up to the church buildings, which were immaculate in appearance. Beautiful lawn. Exquisite stained glass in the foyer. Elegant furnishings. Friendly people who greeted everyone as they arrived. Deep carpet. Original works of art in well-appointed rooms . . . the works. As we stood chatting with the greeters, I couldn't help noticing a long row of tastefully framed oil portraits hanging along the brick wall separating the narthex from the sanctuary. I studied each one. I cannot recall them all, but they included an ancient Greek poet, a British statesman, a famous composer, the late President John F. Kennedy, a renowned winner of the Nobel Peace Prize, Mahatma Ghandi, and Jesus of Nazareth. It was a real mixture of human greatness, fame, and achievement. But what stood out in my mind were the bronze, four-inch letters above the portraits:

FOR YOU ARE ALL SONS OF GOD
Galatians 3:26

After we made our way inside the almost-full sanctuary, I turned to that verse in my Bible. I learned a great deal about the teachings of that church when I observed what had been *omitted* from the quotation of that particular verse of Scripture:

THROUGH FAITH IN CHRIST JESUS.

Don't be sidetracked by other things as you attempt to discern truth from error. Certainly there is nothing wrong with fine buildings, elegant furnishings, works of art, and a well-manicured landscape. But when the name of Christ is deliberately omitted lest things appear "too narrow," it is time to wonder if there might be wolves in sheep's clothing on the loose. Simple faith, as I have said before, is not gullible faith.

Tragically, false teachers lead to false followers, a subject that Jesus addresses next in His discourse.

Two Claims

If you think it has gotten a little tight so far, hold on:

Not everyone who says to Me, "Lord, Lord," will enter the kingdom of heaven; but he who does the will of My

Father who is in heaven. Many will say to Me on that day, "Lord, Lord, did we not prophesy in Your name, and in Your name cast out demons, and in Your name perform many miracles?" And then I will declare to them, "I never knew you; DEPART FROM ME, YOU WHO PRACTICE LAWLESSNESS." Matthew 7:21-23

If you are the religious type who loves creedal affirmations more than biblical application, those words Jesus spoke probably make you nervous. Plenty nervous. They were spoken to get the religious professionals off the fence of theory (where things sound so right, so pious) and into the world of reality (where true Christianity is put into action). Christ, then and now, continues to look for and affirm each person "who does the will of My Father." Not talkers . . . *doers.* Not people who make all the public declarations, but those who walk the talk by living the life. You see, simple faith—a genuine, heartfelt, deep-seated relationship with Jesus Christ, based on faith, not works—soon and often reveals itself in Christlike actions. True believers ultimately do more than believe . . . they demonstrate a life of obedience as their faith is lived out on a day-to-day basis. They are not saved by works, but works do follow their conversion. Works prove the validity of our faith.

Let me go one step further here. The works I refer to are not mere words, important though words are. Jesus Himself spoke condemningly of those who say "Lord,

Lord." He went further and pointed out those who prophesy and perform religious deeds, claiming they do them all in His name; yet He says of them, "I never knew you." Telling us what? That there is a major difference between mouthing the right words or carrying out impressive deeds and being men and women whose hearts have been invaded by the Lord Jesus Christ. The former is religion, the latter, a relationship; the former is surface talk and superficial deed, the latter, an authentic inner transformation brought about through vital faith in Christ.

In summary, Jesus has given us three warnings:

- Only one kind of gate leads to eternal life with God. It is the narrow one, not chosen by the majority.

- Only one kind of teacher deserves to be followed. It is the one who embraces the truth as set forth in Scripture.

- Only one kind of person can have the assurance of eternal life with God. It is the one whose simple faith in Jesus Christ leads to works of obedience.

SIMPLY PUT: A PERSONAL RESPONSE

One—and only one—question ought to consume us at the close of a chapter this direct. *What about me?*

To determine the answer, the following questions may help:

- Have I chosen the correct gate?
- Am I traveling the right road?
- Does my tree bear the right fruit?
- Am I following those who teach the truth?
- Is my faith being demonstrated in good deeds?
- Do I truly know God through Jesus Christ?

I care too much to shield you from the harsh reality of choosing any alternative but Christ. You are free to reject Him and continue to live apart from Him . . . you know that . . . but if you die without Him, all hell will break loose. Literally. Immediately.

It makes no difference whether you have lived a busy life of empty religion full of nice-sounding God talk, or a life entirely devoid of spiritual things. Either way, Jesus declares you are lost. The issue is your lack of a faith relationship with Him.

I urge you, turn to Him now. As you have read, especially in this chapter, He is the only alternative God honors: "the way, the truth, the life."

> Without the way, there is no going
> Without the truth, there is no knowing
> Without the life, there is no living.[6]

Simple faith begins with Christ.

CHAPTER FOURTEEN

The Simple Secret of
an Unsinkable Life

FEW THINGS are more enjoyable than a good story. It makes no difference whether the story is true or fictional, happy or sad, long or short; if it has enough human interest and if the surprise element keeps us dangling, our concentration doesn't waver.

It happened to me just this past week while I was talking with Joe Gibbs, head coach of the Washington Redskins, and he mentioned a funny story that had to do with one of his friends. Since it was true, my interest was immediately tweaked.

Joe's friend owns a fine Labrador retriever. The friend, whom I will call Frank (not his real name), looked out his window one morning and saw his faithful, obedient dog sitting on his haunches near the front porch. Frank thought he saw something hanging from the dog's jaws. Sure enough, a closer look revealed it was his neighbor's pet rabbit . . . now dead. Frank was stunned. Not exactly sure what to do, his brain clicked through several options until he landed on one that seemed the best, though it would require a rather tedious process.

He gingerly pulled the rabbit from the Lab's mouth, brought the thing into the kitchen, and washed off all the dirt and gunk. He then took it into the bathroom, pulled out a hair dryer, and spent several minutes blow-drying the dead creature until it was nice and fluffy. That night, after it was dark and quiet in the neighborhood, Frank crawled over the back fence, slipped across the neighbor's backyard, opened the door on the rabbit hutch, placed the dead rabbit back in the cage, and snapped the door shut. He then slithered back through the darkness, hopped the fence, and breathed a big sigh of relief.

Next morning there was a loud knocking at his front door. Frank opened it and, to his surprise, found his neighbor clutching the dead rabbit. He was steaming.

"Frank, we have a real sickie in our neighborhood."

"Really? Why do you say that?"

"Well, see . . . my rabbit here died three days ago and I buried it. Some guy just dug it up, cleaned it off nice 'n' neat, and *stuck it back in the hutch*. We're talkin' a *real sickie,* Frank!"

Stories stay with us, especially those that sneak past the defenses of the intellect and lodge in the soft, nostalgic places of our heart. We remember not only the people involved in them but the plot that held us in rapt attention the first time we heard the story.

Since my work involves the communication of biblical truth, I often rely on stories from the Scriptures to illustrate what I'm getting at or to drive a point home. They work like magic. I have witnessed one well-placed story from Scripture change the mood of a congregation in less than two minutes. Who wouldn't be interested in a story about true-to-life characters from biblical days whose situation matches today so perfectly? Among my favorites would be:

- David and Goliath
- Daniel in the lion's den
- Joseph forgiving his brothers
- Jonah in the great fish
- Elijah on Mount Carmel
- Samson and Delilah
- Naaman the leper being cleansed
- The plagues in Egypt
- Jacob wrestling with the Angel
- Job's losses and suffering
- Jesus' feeding the 5,000
- The raising of Lazarus
- Paul and Silas in Philippian jail
- Peter walking in water
- Abraham almost sacrificing Isaac on Mount Moriah
- Moses at the Red Sea
- Cain and Abel
- Noah and the ark
- The crucifixion of our Lord
- The empty tomb

The list is endless, of course. Each story captures us with such captivating charm that we relive the account as if we had stepped into a time tunnel and walked where the ancients walked. Try though we may, it becomes impossible to remain aloof from such events.

A good story doesn't permit casual observation. It wraps you up in truth and recognition and won't let go. You are there, in the story; your imagination is kindled; you are involved; you interact with truth on a deep and personal level because you are in the story and now the story is in you. Then it's over, and you sit in the embrace of truth. The story is still resonating in the deepest part of you. For the moment, you are still because it simply takes some time to "get back." And once you emerge from the story, you are never the same again. That's what stories can do.[1]

STORIES THAT STAY WITH US

What is it that makes a good story "stick"? Why, with all the other things we have to think about, do they not get lost from our minds? I think we could boil it down to three reasons:

- People and personalities give a story interest. We soon forget abstract concepts, but never interesting characters.

- Life situations that we can enter into provide scenes with which we can identify. Similar circumstances draw us in. Often, the plot includes a struggle we are going through or a chain of events not unlike something that once happened to us.

- Good stories teach lasting lessons from which we gain new perspective. The best ones, of course, need no explanation. They stand on their own, leaving us pensive and riveted to the seat.

Jesus was a master storyteller. His favorites were parables. Interesting word, *parable;* it means, literally, "to cast alongside." In other words, a parable is a story in which some familiar situation is cast alongside the unfamiliar for the purpose of illustration—making the unfamiliar clear and easy to grasp.

I suppose we could say that the parables Jesus told were profound comparisons in story form. For example? The Prodigal Son. Or the farmer who sowed seed in different soils. Or the lost sheep. Or the Good Samaritan. Wonderful stories, all! He relied on such stories to underscore some particular truth He wanted people to understand, yes—but more importantly, to apply. A life of simple faith is built, I believe, on a reservoir of simple yet profound stories.

So we should not be surprised that when Jesus reached the climactic conclusion of His Sermon on the Mount, He relied on a story to clinch His final words and leave His listeners speechless. Did it work?

The result was that when Jesus had finished these words, the multitudes were amazed at His teaching; for He was teaching them as one having authority, and not as their scribes.   Matthew 7:28–29

For folks who had slept through many a long and

boring sermon, that was saying a lot. To the end they sat spellbound, shaking their heads in amazement, astonished—another vote for profound stories that make the truth stick.

A PARABLE OF LASTING VALUE

Even though the concluding story Jesus told has become familiar to many, let me encourage you to read it as if for the first time. By doing so you will see new vistas and feel a fresh touch from the scene Jesus verbally paints.

> Therefore everyone who hears these words of Mine, and acts upon them, may be compared to a wise man, who built his house upon the rock. And the rain descended, and the floods came, and the winds blew, and burst against that house; and yet it did not fall, for it had been founded upon the rock. And everyone who hears these words of Mine, and does not act upon them, will be like a foolish man, who built his house upon the sand. And the rain descended, and the floods came, and the winds blew, and burst against that house; and it fell, and great was its fall.   Matthew 7:24-27

As I ponder the scene Jesus creates so colorfully with words, I detect at least three categories in the story.

First, *identical elements*. The two main characters are builders. They are building the same things in two different locations: two builders constructing two houses. Let me also hasten to point out that Jesus is not talking about building literal houses on literal rock and literal sand but about building lives—establishing values and determining priorities on contrasting philosophies or lifestyles.

Another set of identical elements in the story is the life situations of both builders. Each goes through a storm. Neither is able to escape it or ignore it. Both feel the downpouring rain that increases to flood level and the sting of the wind that hits with horrendous velocity. Such storms are inevitable. Clearly Jesus is not telling us how to find a safe, comfortable setting, an ideal atmosphere where life remains nonthreatening and where the climate is wonderfully supportive. On the contrary, His story is forcing us to face reality: life is difficult . . . storms are inevitable . . . pain and discomfort happen. As Earl Palmer says:

> We must prepare the houses we are building for wind, rain, and floods. We must prepare the child for the road, not the road for the child. There is a testing of all of the houses we are building, and that testing is built into the whole plan; no favorites are excused from the inevitable testing of the value systems and philosophies of life and dreams into which we invest our lives.[2]

There is no escaping life's calamities.

The second category is *contrasting factors.* The two builders may be constructing identical houses and the same storm may be blasting both places with similar fury, but the builders themselves are totally different kinds of men. That means they build their houses in to-tally different manners. One chooses to build on rock; the other, on sand. The first builder is the type who does more than hear what Christ has to say. According to Jesus' own words, he hears and acts upon the truth. Interestingly, the second builder hears the very same things . . . but he stops there. He deliberately does not act upon what he hears. Jesus called the first builder "wise" and the second builder "foolish." Curiously, no one can tell by looking at the builders which one hears and acts and which one merely hears. It takes a storm to reveal which is which.

A second contrast in the story is eloquent—the ultimate outcome of the two houses. One "did not fall"; the other "fell, and great was its fall." The wise builder has so constructed his life that no amount of testing, no extent of difficulty, is sufficient to bring him down. Why? The story line tells us it is because "it had been founded upon the rock." It takes no theologian to identify what the rock represents . . . Christ Himself. The wise builder has turned to the Lord Jesus Christ in simple faith and, acting upon the truth He teaches, has built his life on the principles of His instruction. This gives him a solid and secure foundation unlike his counterpart, whose life is foolishly built on sand. This, of course, is the story that gave birth to a gospel song the church has sung for over a century:

> My hope is built on nothing less
> Than Jesus' blood and righteousness;

I dare not trust the sweetest frame,
But wholly lean on Jesus' name.

On Christ, the solid Rock, I stand;
All other ground is sinking sand,
All other ground is sinking sand.

The third category is *underlying principles.* As I think through the story, two enduring principles emerge:

1. If you are only hearing and reading the truth, you are not prepared for life's storms.

Throughout the pages of this book I have reiterated the importance of embracing truth, not just hearing it or thinking about it. In this information era it is easy for us to become fascinated by more and more words, interested in intriguing concepts—and making the process of gathering data an end in itself rather than acting upon the truth that is presented. The "foolish" builder heard everything the "wise" builder heard. The only difference was his refusal to do something about it. Small wonder Jesus frequently punctuated His remarks with the reminder "He who has ears to hear, let him hear!" To listen with no plan to act—to read with no interest in responding—is to miss the whole point of Christ's great message on the mountain. Divine truth is given not to satisfy idle curiosity, but to change lives . . . not to lull us to sleep in church, but to equip us for today and ready us for eternity.

Charles Spurgeon was gravely concerned about this over a hundred years ago:

> There are tens of thousands to whom the preaching of the gospel is as music in the ears of a corpse. They shut their ears and will not hear, though the testimony be concerning God's own Son, and life eternal, and the way to escape from everlasting wrath. To their own best interests, to their eternal benefit, men are dead; nothing will secure their attention to their God. To what, then, are these men like? They may fitly be compared to the man who built no house whatever, and remained homeless by day and shelterless by night. When worldly trouble comes like a storm those persons who will not hear the words of Jesus have no consolation to cheer them; when sickness comes they have no joy of heart to sustain them under its pains; and when death, that most terrible of storms, beats upon them they feel its full fury, but they cannot find a hiding place. *They neglect the housing of their souls,* and when the hurricane of almighty wrath shall break forth in the world to come they will have no place of refuge. In vain will they call upon the rocks to fall upon them, and the mountains to cover them. They shall be in that day without a shelter from the righteous wrath of the Most High.[3] (emphasis mine)

Be certain that you have *acted upon* the truth not just read colorful words and interacted with mentally stimulating concepts.

2. If your foundation is sure, no storm will cause your life to collapse.

The rains of adversity will fall, no question about it. That's life. The floods of misery and heartache will rise, for sure. No one can dodge such harsh realities. And the winds of pressure will howl, threatening both your security and your sanity. As one of my mentors used to say, "Hardship is part of the divine curriculum: Reality 101." But the good news is this: Your life will not collapse. Christ came to be believed in, not simply studied and admired.

There is a moving story of Steinberg and the gypsy girl. Struck with her beauty, Steinberg took her to his studio and frequently had her sit for him. At that time he was at work on his masterpiece "Christ on the Cross." The girl used to watch him work on this painting. One day she said to him, "He must have been a very wicked man to be nailed to a cross like that." "No," said the painter. "On the contrary, he was a very good man. The best man that ever lived. He died for others." The little girl looked up at him and asked, "Did he die for you?" Steinberg was not a Christian, but the gypsy girl's question touched his heart and awakened his conscience, and he became a believer in him whose dying passion he had so well portrayed. Years afterward a young count chanced to go into the gallery at Dresden where Steinberg's painting of "Christ on the Cross" was on exhibition. This painting spoke so powerfully to him that it changed the whole tenor of his life. He was Count Nikolaus von Zinzendorf, founder of the Moravian Brethren.[4]

The great sermon Jesus preached on the mountain has not been preserved simply because it is a literary masterpiece. It is here to be acted upon. We are to step into it, make its truths our own, and in doing so, discover the simple secret of an unsinkable life. That means building on the right foundation . . . the solid Rock of Christ rather than the sinking sands of a self-made life.

SIMPLY PUT: TWO LINGERING QUESTIONS AND A LOVE STORY

I have so enjoyed spending time with you in the pages of this book. We have shared similar emotions as we have pushed aside all the clutter of religious activity and returned to many of the basics of simple faith.

But as enjoyable as our time together has been, I must confess that I am concerned. Since I cannot sit down beside you, look at you, speak with you, and listen to you, I have no way of knowing whether these have been mere words you have read or truths you now embrace by faith. My hope, of course, is the latter.

Two lingering questions are yours—and only yours—to answer:

- Is the foundation beneath your life absolutely solid? If it is on Christ, the Rock, it is. If not, it isn't.

- Is the life you are building eternally reliable? Storms are sure to come, bringing a downpour of

difficulties that will test the materials you are
using. If your life is solidly and squarely resting
on Christ, you will ride out the storm, not
fearing the flood. If not, the sand will ultimately
give way, your life will collapse, and you will sink.

Admittedly the last two chapters of my book have
been direct and pointed. You may even think I have
seemed a little too severe. You must understand that I
write out of great passion . . . and perhaps in doing
so, I have failed to communicate a dimension of the living God that makes His message so appealing. It is His
love. He does not stand aloof from us, pointing and
shouting words of condemnation. Rather, He reaches
back to us with open arms, offering His strength in
place of our weakness. He desires to help us in our
struggles, to rescue us from sinking, and to bring us to
safety. I repeat, it is His all-conquering love that refuses to let us sink and drown.

The truth of all this is brought home beautifully in
one of Frederick Buechner's poignant volumes, *The
Wizard's Tide.* There he writes of young Teddy
Schroeder and his sister Bean, who grew up in the disastrous era of the Great Depression. It is the "mostly
true story" (as Buechner puts it) of a family struggling
to find harmony and love amidst those turbulent times.

Out of that story, one particular scene comes to
mind. Teddy and his family, including his grandpar-
ents, were enjoying some time together at the beach.

For Teddy, the best part of the day was his chance to go swimming in the ocean with his father. They rode the waves together for a while before his father told him he felt the boy was ready to swim out to the barrels. The barrels were a long distance from shore, and only the stronger, more experienced swimmers even attempted to go that far, since they were anchored out there to show that it was not safe to swim beyond them. To Teddy, they seemed frighteningly far.

Off splashed father and son through the salty ocean waves. When they were about halfway . . .

Teddy thought the barrels still looked a long way off, and the beach was so far behind he could hardly recognize his mother and Bean sitting on it. His arms were beginning to ache, and he was feeling out of breath. What if he started to drown, he thought? What if he called for help and his father, who was a little ahead of him didn't hear? What if a giant octopus swam up from below and wrapped him in its slimy green tentacles?

But just as he was thinking these things, his father turned around and treaded water, waiting for him.

"How about a lift the rest of the way?" Mr. Schroeder said. So Teddy paddled over and put his arms around his father's neck from behind, and that was the best part of the day for him and the part he remembered for many years afterward.

He remembered how the sunlight flashed off his father's freckly, wet shoulders and the feel of the muscles working inside them as he swam. He remembered the back of his father's head and the way his ears looked from behind and the way his hair stuck out over them. He remembered how his father's hair felt thick and wiry like a horse's mane against his cheek and how he tried not to hold on to his neck too tightly for fear he'd choke him.

His mother said bad things about his father. She said that he had no get-up-and-go and that he was worse than Grandpa Schroeder already though thirty years younger. She said he needed a swift kick in the pants and things like that. And Teddy knew that his father did things that he wished he wouldn't, like drink too many cocktails and drive his car up on the lawn and come to kiss him and Bean goodnight with his face all clammy and cold.

But as he swam out toward the barrels on his father's back, he also knew that there was no place in the whole Atlantic ocean where he felt so safe.[5]

It was while picturing that scene in my mind that the words of the old gospel song took on new life:

I was sinking deep in sin, far from the peaceful shore,
Very deeply stained within, sinking to rise no more;
But the Master of the sea heard my despairing cry,
From the waters lifted me, now safe am I.

Love lifted me! Love lifted me!
When nothing else could help,
Love lifted me.[6]

All of us who now live in simple faith were once rescued from sinking sand.

Conclusion

AMONG THE MANY plays and musical performances I have attended, none has ever gripped me like *Les Misérables*. When these playwrights and composers decided to put Victor Hugo's classic novel on the stage in the form of a dramatic musical, a masterpiece was created for the public to enjoy. When my family and I saw the performance, we were moved to tears . . . literally. To this day, its scenes and songs often return to mind, bringing fresh delight.

As you may know *Les Misérables* is another story of a lifelong conflict between law and grace . . . between one whose hatred and bitterness drove him to despair and another, reclaimed by forgiveness, who chose to live in love and grace.

Jean Valjean, released on parole after nineteen years on the chain gang, soon learns that his wretched past has condemned him to the life of an outcast. Only a saintly bishop treats him kindly; and yet Valjean, scarred and hardened by his prison years, repays the bishop by stealing some of his silver. Caught and brought back by the police, Valjean is astonished when the bishop demonstrates mercy and lies to the authorities to save him. In addition, the kind man of God forgives him, extends love to him, and gives him two precious silver candlesticks. Seized with the significance of such an act of grace, Valjean declares that he will never be the same. He will become a man of simple faith and begin to live a worthwhile life.

From then on, however, Valjean is hunted and haunted by his enemy, the policeman Javert, who is determined to prove him guilty and get him back into prison. Valjean, nevertheless, stays with his commitment. In utter humility, he refuses to retaliate, which both infuriates and confuses Javert, the consummate legalist. In tender love, Valjean adopts the child Cosette and later risks his life for her fiancé. Again and again, he overcomes evil with good by turning the other cheek, loving his neighbor as himself, refusing to seek his own needs first, sacrificing for those in need, and doing unto others as he would have them do unto him. Consistently, he shakes salt and shines light, never bears grudges, continues to care for the dying, and, in the end, overpowers his enemy, Javert, with the love of Christ. In short, Jean Valjean models the Sermon on the Mount.

The last line of the theater production captures both the essence of the musical and the message of this book: "To love another person is to see the face of God."

In a busy, angry, complicated world like ours, I know of no greater need than an authentic display of simple faith. Surrounded by a jumble of activities being carried out by exhausted, joyless people–many of them claiming to be Christians–the presence of a life that demonstrates love and extends grace, a life that represents compassion, humility, and mercy, is long overdue. Because Jesus did so in His days on earth, the impact was astounding. It was, in fact, life-changing. The world awaits others, who, like Jean Valjean, will walk as He walked, forgive as He forgave, care as He cared, love as He loved.

Will you be one of them?

In the hurried lives of too many Christians there is a *peace* missing. We will not find it until we return to the only life worth living . . . a life of simple faith.

Notes

Introduction

1 From the hymn "And Can It Be That I Should Gain?"
   by Charles Wesley (1707–88).

Chapter One   Let's Keep It Simple

1 Larry Hein, quoted by Brennan Manning, *Lion and
   Lamb* (Old Tappan, N.J.: Chosen Books, Fleming H.
   Revell Co., 1986), 24.
2 Lewis Sperry Chafer, quoted in Richard H. Seume,
   Shoes for the Road (Chicago, Ill.: Moody Press, 1974),
   44.
3 From *The Churchman,* Diocese of Dallas, quoted in
   Charles Allen, *You Are Never Alone* (Old Tappan,
   N.J.: Fleming H. Revell Co., 1978), 143–44.
4 Archibald Thomas Robertson, *Word Pictures in the
   New Testament,* vol. 1 (Nashville, Tenn.: Broadman
   Press, 1930), 63.
5 Robert A. Raines, *Creative Brooding* (New York:
   Macmillan Publishing Co., 1966), 94–95.

6   Arthur Bennett, ed., *The Valley of Vision* (Carlisle, Pa.: The Banner of Truth Trust, 1975), 91.

Chapter Two   The Qualities of Simple Faith

1   G. K. Chesterton, *The Everlasting Man* (New York: Doubleday, 1974), 194–95.
2   From "Rock of Ages," Augustus Toplady (1776).
3   D. Martyn Lloyd-Jones, *Studies in the Sermon on the Mount,* 2 vols. (Grand Rapids, Mich.: William B. Eerdmans Publishing Co., 1959–62), 1:69.
4   Robertson, *Word Pictures,* 41.
5   John R. W. Stott, *Christian Counter-Culture: The Message of the Sermon on the Mount* (Downers Grove, Ill.: InterVarsity Press, 1978), 49.
6   Dietrich Bonhoeffer, *The Cost of Discipleship* (New York: Collier Books, Macmillan Publishing Co., 1963), 45ff.
7   Ibid., 121.
8   J. B. Phillips, *Good News: Thoughts on God and Man* (New York: Macmillan Co., 1963), 33–34.
9   Ibid., 34.

Chapter Three   A Simple Counterstrategy: Shake and Shine

1   Lloyd-Jones, *Studies in the Sermon,* 1:37.
2   Earl F. Palmer, *The Enormous Exception* (Waco, Tex.: Word Books, 1986), 33–34.
3   Norman P. Grubb, *C. T. Studd: Cricketer and Pioneer* (Philadelphia, Pa.: Christian Literature Crusade, 1948), 166.
4   Stott, *Christian Counter-Culture,* 61.

5   Bennett, *The Valley of Vision*, 1.
6   Rebecca Manley Pippert, *Out of the Saltshaker*
    (Downers Grove, Ill.: InterVarsity Press, 1979), 162.

Chapter Four   Simplicity Starts from Within

1   D. Martyn Lloyd-Jones, *Preaching and Preachers*
    (Grand Rapids, Mich.: Zondervan Publishing House,
    1971), 97.
2   Ibid., 320.
3   Billy Graham, *Facing Death and the Life After*
    (Waco, Tex.: Word Books, 1987), 174.

*Chapter Five   Simple Instructions on
              Serious Issues*

1   Paul O'Neil, quoted in George P. Hunt, "Editor's
    Note: Attila the Hun in a Tattered Sweater," *Life*, 13
    November 1964, 3.
2   James T. Fisher, quoted in Charles L. Allen, *The
    Sermon on the Mount* (Westwood, N.J.: Fleming H.
    Revell Co., 1966), 18.
3   C.S. Lewis, *Mere Christianity* (New York: Macmillan
    Co., 1958), 106.
4   William Whiston, trans., *Josephus' Complete Works*
    (Grand Rapids, Mich.: Kregel Publications, 1960),
    99.
5   Stott, *Christian Counter-Culture*, 94–95. I am
    indebted to John R. W. Stott for his excellent devel-
    opment of these three observations.
6   Philip Schaff, ed., *Saint Chrysostom: Homilies on the
    Gospel of St. Matthew*, vol. 10 of *A Select Library of
    the Nicene and Post-Nicene Fathers of the Christian*

Church (Grand Rapids, Mich.: William B. Eerdmans Publishing Co., 1983), 119.

7 Billy Kim, quoted in Stuart Briscoe, *Now for Something Totally Different* (Waco, Tex.: Word Books, 1978), 100–101.

8 Lloyd H. Steffen, "On Honesty and Self-Deception: '*You Are the Man,*'" *The Christian Century,* 29 April 1987.

Chapter Six   Simple Advice to the Selfish and Strong-Willed

1 Sam Vincent Meddis, "7 Cities Lead Violence 'Epidemic,'" *USA Today,* 29 April 1991.

2 William Barclay, *The Gospel of Matthew,* vol. 1 (Philadelphia: Westminster Press, 1975), 163.

3 Stott, *Christian Counter-Culture,* 108.

4 Barclay, *Matthew,* 171–72.

5 A. F. C. Vilmar, cited in Dietrich Bonhoeffer, *The Cost of Discipleship* (New York: Collier Books, Macmillan Publishing Co., 1963), 167–69.

6 Alfred Plummer, *An Exegetical Commentary on the Gospel According to St. Matthew* (London: Robert Scott Roxburghe House, 1909), 89.

Chapter Seven   Beware! Religious Performance Now Showing

1 C. S. Lewis, *The Weight of Glory* (New York: Macmillan Publishing Co., 1980), 4.

2 Paul Tournier, *Secrets* (New York: Pillar Publications, 1976), 22, 29.

3   Robert Robinson, "Come, Thou Fount," adapted by
    Margaret Clarkson.

*Chapter Eight • Prayer and Fasting Minus All
    the Pizzazz*

1   Lloyd-Jones, *Studies in the Sermon,* 2:13.
2   Palmer, *The Enormous Exception,* 145.
3   Barclay, *Matthew,* 236.

Chapter Nine   When Simple Faith Erodes

1   Oswald Chambers, *My Utmost for His Highest* (New
    York: Dodd, Mead and Co., 1952), 110.
2   Martin Luther, cited in Stott, *Christian Counter-
    Culture,* 155.
3   Lloyd-Jones, *Studies in the Sermon,* 2:98.
4   Ibid., 97–106.
5   David J. Beattie, *The Romance of Sacred Song* (Lon-
    don: Marshall, Morgan, and Scott, 1931), 216–17.
6   Robinson, "Come, Thou Fount," adapted by
    Margaret Clarkson.

Chapter Ten   The Subtle Enemy of Simple Faith

1   Jason Lehman, "Present Tense." Used by permission.
2   Clarence Edward Macartney, *Macartney's Illustra-
    tions* (New York: Abingdon-Cokesbury Press, 1946),
    414.
3   Ben Patterson, *The Grand Essentials* (Waco, Tex.:
    Word Books, 1987), 35.
4   Ibid., 144.

Chapter Eleven   If You're Serious About Simple
            Faith, Stop This!

1   Told in slightly different form in Charles R. Swindoll,
     Three Steps Forward, Two Steps Back (Nashville,
     Tenn.: Thomas Nelson Publishers, 1980), 25–27.
2   Barclay, *Matthew,* 261–62.
3   Charles Haddon Spurgeon, *The King Has Come,* ed.
     Larry O. Richards (Old Tappan, N.J.: Fleming H.
     Revell Co., 1987), 78.

Chapter Twelve   The Most Powerful of All Four-
            Letter Words

1   J. B. Phillips, *Making Men Whole* (London: Collins,
     1955), 75.
2   D. A. Carson, *The Sermon on the Mount: An Evan-*
     gelical Exposition of Matthew 5–7 (Grand Rapids,
     Mich.: Baker Book House, 1978), 109.
3   From "The Gospel According to You" in *Poems That*
     Preach, comp. John R. Rice (Wheaton, Ill.: Sword of
     the Lord Publishers, 1952), 68.

Chapter Thirteen   Simple Yet Serious Warnings
            for Complicated Times

1   Condensed from Tom Parker, *In One Day: The*
     Things Americans Do in a Day (Boston: Houghton
     Mifflin Co., 1984).
2   Virginia Brasier, "Time of the Mad Atom," as quoted
     in Sara Brewton, John E. Brewton, and John Brewton
     Blackburn, *Of Quarks, Quasars, and Other Quirks:*
     Quizzical Poems for the Supersonic Age (New York:
     Thomas Y. Crowell Co., 1977), 2.

3 Lloyd-Jones, *Studies in the Sermon,* 2:218-19.

4 C. S. Lewis, *Surprised by Joy* (New York: Harcourt, Brace and World, 1955), 60.

5 William Pringle, trans., *Commentary on a Harmony of the Evangelists, Matthew, Mark and Luke,* vol. 1 (Grand Rapids, Mich.: Baker Book House, 1984), 365.

6 Merrill Tenney, *John: The Gospel of Belief* (Grand Rapids, Mich.: William B. Eerdmans Publishing Co., 1948), 215-16.

Chapter Fourteen   The Simple Secret of an Unsinkable Life

1 Reg Grant and John Reed, *Telling Stories to Touch the Heart* (Wheaton, Ill.: Victor Books, 1990), 9.

2 Palmer, *The Enormous Exception,* 143.

3 Charles Haddon Spurgeon, "On Laying Foundations," in vol. 29 of *Metropolitan Tabernacle Pulpit* (London: Banner of Truth, 1971), 49-50.

4 Clarence Edward Macartney, *Preaching Without Notes* (New York: Abingdon Press, 1946), 45.

5 Frederick Buechner, *The Wizard's Tide* (San Francisco: Harper & Row, 1990), 45-46.

6 "Love Lifted Me," James Rowe (1865-1935).

The author gratefully acknowledges the following writers and publishers for permission to quote from their works:

The Valley of Vision, a collection of Puritan prayers, ed. Arthur Bennett. Copyright 1975 by Banner of Truth Trust. Used by permission of the publisher.

Selections from Dietrich Bonhoeffer, *The Cost of*

Discipleship, trans. R. H. Fuller, with some revision by Irmgard Booth (New York: Macmillan; London: SCM Press, 1959). Reprinted by permission of the publisher.

"Time of the Mad Atom," by Virginia Brasier, © 1949. Reprinted with permission of the *Saturday Evening Post*.

An untitled poem from Norman Grubb, *C. T. Studd, Cricketer & Pioneer* (Fort Washington, Pa.: Christian Literature Crusade; Cambridge: Lutterworth Press, 1933). Used by permission.

"Present Tense," a poem by Jason Lehman, 36 Old Quarry Road, Woodbridge, Conn. 06525. Used by permission.

Creative Brooding, by Robert A. Raines. Copyright 1966 by Macmillan Publishing Company, Inc. Reprinted by permission of the publisher.

"The Gospel According to You" in *Poems That Preach*, comp. John R. Rice (Wheaton, Ill.: Sword of the Lord Publishers, 1952), 68. Used by permission of the publisher.

Lloyd H. Steffen, "On Honesty and Self-Deception: 'You Are the Man,'" *The Christian Century*, 29 April 1987. Used by permission of the Christian Century Foundation.

ABOUT THE AUTHOR

CHARLES R. SWINDOLL serves as president of Dallas Theological Seminary. He is also president of Insight for Living, a radio broadcast ministry aired daily worldwide. He was senior pastor at the First Evangelical Free Church in Fullerton, California for almost twenty-three years and has authored numerous books on Christian living, including the best-selling *The Grace Awakening, Laugh Again,* and *Flying Closer to the Flame.*